Writing *Strands*

A COMPLETE WRITING PROGRAM
USING A PROCESS APPROACH
TO WRITING AND COMPOSITION

ASSURING
CONTINUITY AND CONTROL

LEVEL 7

of
a complete writing program
for homeschoolers

a
publication
of

NATIONAL WRITING INSTITUTE
624 W. University #248
Denton, TX 76201-1889

ISBN10: 1-888344-07-5
ISBN13:978-1-888344-07-3

Manufactured in the United States of America

For information, write: National Writing Institute
                          624 W. University #248
                          Denton, TX 76201-1889

                          call: 1 (800) 688-5375
                          e-mail: info@writingstrands.com

NATIONAL WRITING INSTITUTE PUBLICATIONS

STUDENTS

Writing Strands Level 1
Writing Strands Level 2
Writing Strands Level 3
Writing Strands Level 4
Writing Strands Level 5
Writing Strands Level 6
Writing Strands Level 7
Writing Exposition
Creating Fiction

Communication And Interpersonal Relationships

___

PARENTS/TEACHERS

Evaluating Writing
Reading Strands

___

INTRODUCTION

This group of exercises is designed to give seventh level students (generally advanced high school students, if they haven't used *Writing Strands* or any student who has completed the sixth level of *Writing Strands*) an introduction to the very complicated process of giving others their thoughts in written form.

The learning of this skill is one of the hardest jobs that you have. These exercises will make it easier. Much of the planning and detail of the writing process is presented here.

The writing exercises in this level are in three categories: creative, research and report, and expository. The exercises in each of these areas will guide you in the development of the skills you'll need.

Rather than increase the work for your parents, this writing process should make it easier for both you and your parents to meet the demands for more student writing.

These exercises are not presented as the ultimate answer. They're detailed suggestions. If the exercises are attempted and you work hard, you'll have a well-founded introduction to this most difficult skill, and your parents will find it easier to have confidence that this part of the teaching challenge has been met.

CONTENTS

How To Make *Writing Strands* **Work For You** i
Principles ii
Exercises * Skills * Objectives . . . . iii-v
Strands vi
Not Rules, More Like Suggestions vii
Stuff I Learned Last Year I Feel Really Good About viii

Exercise #1 **What Our Feet Do** (Creative) 1
    Progress Report For Exercise #1 7

Exercise #2 **If I Were A**. . . (Research and Report) 8
    Progress Report For Exercise #2 15

Exercise #3 **Describing Characters** (Creative) 16
    Progress Report For Exercise #3 20

Exercise #4 **Conflic**t (Creative) 21
    Progress Report For Exercise #4 26

Exercise #5 **Point Of View** (Expository) 27
    Progress Report For Exercise #5 37

Exercise #6 **What Makes It What It Is** (Creative) 38
    Progress Report For Exercise #6 42

Exercise #7 **Survey** (Research) 43
    Progress Report For Exercise #7 48

Exercise #8 **Argumen**t (Expository) 49
    Progress Report For Exercise #8 58

Spelling List 59
First Semester Report 60

Exercise #9 **Book Report** (Research and Report) 62
    Progress Report For Exercise #9 63

Exercise #10 **Behavior** (Report) 64
    Progress Report For Exercise #10 69

Exercise #11 **Interview With A Character** (Creative) 70
    Progress Report For Exercise #11 75

Exercise #12 **Problems** (Creative) 76
    Progress Report For Exercise #12 79

Exercise #13 **Interactions** (Creative) 80
    Progress Report For Exercise #13 84

Exercise #14 **He Did It First** (Creative) 85
    Progress Report For Exercise #14 88

Second Semester Report 89-90
Listing Of Common Problems 91-101

HOW TO MAKE

WRITING STRANDS WORK FOR YOU

1. You should have a writing folder containing all of your written work which should be saved for next year. This will give you a place to store and record your progress, and it's a great thing for your parents to keep.

2. Both semesters' work have evaluations by your parents which may be used if your parents have to have a conference with your local school administration. They contain:

    A. The objectives you have mastered this year;

    B. A place for your parents to comment on your work and a place to list the things you have yet to learn.

3. Each exercise begins with a suggested time for completion. Of course, all students work at different rates. The suggested daily activities can be combined or extended depending on your performance and your parents' schedules.

4. Many of the exercises suggest that your parents will work with you during your schooling period reading what you have written. If this is done, it will serve two purposes:

    A. It will give you constant feedback and will allow your parents to catch many writing problems before they appear in your final papers.

    B. It will greatly cut down on your parents' correcting time outside of your working periods. Most of the paper reading can be done while you're working on language arts, so, even though you'll be writing much more than you previously have been, your parents should be able to help you more using even less outside time.

5. At the end of each semester's work there is an evaluation form that should list the continuing problems you have:

    A. The form at the end of the first semester should contain a listing of the problems that you should work on during the second semester.

    B. The year's-end evaluation form should list the problems that you'll be able to solve next year.

PRINCIPLES

The following principles were adopted by the National Writing Institute before work began on *Writing Strands*. They were our guides in the initial stages of the design of the exercises.

1. Every person needs to learn to express ideas and feelings through writing.

2. There is no one right way to write anything.

3. The ability to write is not an expression of a body of knowledge that can be learned like a list of vocabulary words.

4. Writing teachers and their students both learn in any effective writing situation.

5. The product of each student's writing efforts must be seen as a success for at least the following reasons:

    A. A student in a writing experience is not in competition with anyone else.

    B. There is no perfect model against which any effort can be compared for evaluation, so there is no best way for any student to write.

    C. Every controlled writing experience will help students improve the ability to express themselves.

6. All student writing efforts are worthy of praise. The most help any writing teacher can give at any point is to show, in a positive way, what is good about a piece and how it might be improved.

7. Any writing lesson assigned, which is done independently by a student and doesn't have a teacher's constant feedback in the form of reinforcement and suggestions, represents a missed opportunity for the student.

8. All writing at any level is hard work, and every writer should be encouraged to feel the pride of authorship.

9. All authors need to be published. This can be accomplished by having their work read to family members, posted on the bulletin board, printed in "books" or stuck on the front of the refrigerator.

SEVENTH LEVEL

EXERCISES * SKILLS * OBJECTIVES

Exercise 1: **What Our Feet Do**
Skill Area: Creative

1. Understanding that people vary in the ways they move their bodies
2. Realizing that writers understand this and use it in their writing
3. Using this understanding in writing

Exercise 2: **If I Were A. . .**
Skill Area: Research and Report

1. Understanding that the things we call good and bad (our attitudes) are determined by who we are
2. Accepting that ideas may be looked at in more than one way
3. Understanding that the organization of a report should help the reader understand it

Exercise 3: **Describing Characters**
Skill Area: Creative

1. Realizing that authors can choose what they describe
2. Understanding that authors make these choices to tell their readers what they want them to know
3. Being able to select what to describe and giving the reader that necessary information

Exercise 4: **Conflict**
Skill Area: Creative

1. Understanding that conflicts are important and resolvable
2. Creating and resolving conflicts in writing

Exercise 5: **Point Of View**
Skill Area: Expository

1. Knowing the choices an author has in his use of point of view
2. Understanding how these point of view elements work
3. Understanding the structuring of an explanatory exposition
4. Writing an explanatory exposition

Exercise 6: **What Makes It What It Is**
Skill Area: Creative

1. Creating, for a reader, the character of a place
2. Making a reader feel about a place in a selected way

Exercise 7: **Survey**
Skill Area: Research and Report

1. Writing unbiased questions
2. Selecting a representative sample of respondents for a survey
3. Taking an oral survey
4. Reporting on the results of a survey

Exercise 8: **Argument**
Skill Area: Expository

1. Establishing a position on a local controversial issue
2. Interviewing local experts on an issue
3. Using quotations from experts to support a position
4. Writing an argumentative exposition supporting a chosen position

Exercise 9: **Book Report**
Skill Area: Research and Report

1. Understanding that many novels are based on the development of characters
2. Realizing that characters can be analyzed the same way they're created
3. Writing a book report based on character development

Exercise 10: **Behavior**
Skill Area: Research and Report

   1. Observing a situation and taking notes so as to be able to write about it
   2. Describing what is seen over a period of days
   3. Writing a formal scientific report

Exercise 11: **Interview With A Character**
Skill Area: Research and Report

   1. Understanding that imaginary characters sometimes do what they want to do
   2. Writing an interview

Exercise 12: **Problems**
Skill Strand: Creative

   1. Describing a problem by giving that problem to a character
   2. Creating character motivation
   3. Creating a character with a problem and showing a reader that character working with that problem

Exercise 13: **Interactions**
Skill Area: Creative

   1. Creating an emotional relationship between characters
   2. Punctuating dialogue
   3. Describing, in a dialogue, characters' major body movements caused by their emotional reactions

Exercise 14: **He Did It First**
Skill Area: Creative

   1. Creating a character to be like someone you know
   2. Creating character motivation
   3. Learning about how people handle themselves by working at your writing

STRANDS

Two of the most desired characteristics of any writing program are for it to allow for continuity of instruction from level to level and to allow for control of the learning process by the teacher.

Below are the strands, the exercises that present the strands and where they're found in this text.

Creative   Page

Exercise #1 What Our Feet Do   1
Exercise #3 Describing Characters   16
Exercise #4 Conflict   21
Exercise #6 What Makes It What It Is   38
Exercise #11 Interview With A Character   70
Exercise #12 Problems   76
Exercise #13 Interactions   80
Exercise #14 He Did It First   85

Research/Report

Exercise #2 If I Were A.   8
Exercise #7 Survey   43
Exercise #9 Book Report   62
Exercise #10 Behavior   64

Expository

Exercise #5 Point Of View (Explanatory)   27
Exercise #8 Argument (Argumentative)   49

NOT RULES,

MORE LIKE SUGGESTIONS

In almost everything we do, there are rules (like laws), and then there are what we call "rules." The rules that are like laws are written and we all accept these as the rules we have to live by. Then there are the "rules," the things that we *should* do, that we agree to do, and things that make life nicer for everyone if we do them.

This is also true in writing. As an example of the difference in the rules of writing, look at the rule (law) that says that every sentence must start with a capital letter. This is written down and we all must write using this rule. A "rule" of writing is that we use an exclamation point only once a year.

The following "rules" are just strong suggestions. You can violate them if you want to. It might be good to keep in mind however, that if you do, your readers will look at your writing the same way that the company at dinner might look at you if you burped at the end of the meal. So, below is a short list of the "rules" of writing:

1. Don't use exclamation points! This makes any writing look amateurish and fuzzy. If you're saying something that's important, the way you say it should be strong enough so that you don't have to tell your reader that it's important by using exclamation points at the end of your sentences.

2. Don't underline the titles of your papers. The only time there should be an underline in one of your titles is when you use the names of books or magazines.

3. Skip a line after the title in any paper you're giving to someone else to read.

4. Never write *The End* at the end of anything you write for a schooling exercise.

5. Don't try writing humor until you've studied it and really know the difference between being funny and being corny. (Those places in this book where I've tried to be funny and was corny will give you an example of what I mean.)

6. Don't skip a line between paragraphs.

7. Leave a margin on all sides of every page, and always at the bottom.

8. Check your papers for clichés before you write the final drafts.

STUFF I LEARNED LAST YEAR ABOUT WRITING
THAT I FEEL REALLY GOOD ABOUT

1. _____

   _____

2. _____

   _____

3. _____

   _____

4. _____

   _____

5. _____

   _____

6. _____

   _____

7. _____

   _____

8. _____

   _____

#1 WHAT OUR FEET DO

Skill Strand: Creative

It may take you six days to learn that:
1. People vary in the ways they move their bodies
2. Writers understand these differences
3. You can use this understanding when you create characters

PREWRITING

Day One:

One thing that most people learn as they get older is how to control their body movements. We all had to learn how to do this, and it does take practice to know exactly what the parts of our bodies are doing.

If you were to watch young children, you'd notice they're always moving some part of their bodies, and that this movement has little to do with what they're saying or with what they want to do.

It would be hard for you to find a young child not making random movements with his hands, fingers, arms or legs. This is okay, we all have done this in our process of growing up. Some adults still have difficulty with holding themselves still. But, most of them can sit quietly for long periods of time and not show signs of impatience.

In this exercise you'll create two characters: one who will be able control random body movements, and one who will have some difficulty when upset controlling what goes on with fingers, feet, arms, and hands.

This exercise has three parts:
1. Improvisation and planning
2. Writing
3. Acting

PART ONE: Improvisation and planning

Improvisation is constructing or acting without previous planning. One of your parents might help you do this exercise. Together you'll act out a scene of two people in conversation. One will be an adult who has control of body actions and the other will not have such good control. These two characters will demonstrate their respective (each their own in the order given) abilities to control their bodies. This means that whichever one of you plays the character who has control of body movements will have to control what your body is doing, and the member playing the character who has little control over nervous energy, as it moves body muscles, will have to demonstrate random body movements for that age level.

You and your parent will have to discuss and then decide on a situation for your improvisation. Keep in mind that you're to improvise the actions and speeches of your characters. This means that you and your parent cannot plan exactly what will be said or what will be done in your skit. You'll be able to plan the situation the two characters are in but not what happens.

You should agree on a situation that will show the difference between the characters' abilities to control their bodies. I suggest situations such as the following:

- A woman talking to her neighbor who doesn't want to let on that there is to be a surprise party this evening for her husband

- A mother and her son waiting to be waited upon in a shoe store

- A young person working on a first job who has to explain to the boss that the cash register is short fourteen dollars and fifty cents

- A mother asking her son about why the boy won't take out the garbage on his own

Once you and your parent have chosen a situation, you should act it out. Keep in mind that this exercise is about body control. You should have each character speak at least fifteen to twenty times. This will give you ample time to demonstrate their respective body-control abilities.

You'll not have to resolve any conflict in this short skit. It will not have to have any specific structure. The intent is to give you experience in creating characters who move their bodies in different ways.

After you have run through the improvisation, you're to do it again. This time you're to take notes on what you're doing with your bodies. An easy way to take notes while doing this is to use a tape recorder. As you improvise (in the skit) you can make notes

2

into the recorder and transcribe them later.

Preparation:

(I don't know what else to call it. I thought of "schoolwork, aftersession work, homework" and "prep-work," but none of them worked as well as "preparation." So, if this is new to you, you'll just have to suffer the use of this word.) Both of you will practice your parts and your control of your bodies, and you'll both be ready to do the skit again and to take further notes.

Day Two:

You're to run through the skit again and take notes on body movements. You both could practice different movements—looking for the kinds that are most typical for your age-group/characters.

PART TWO:

WRITING

Preparation:

You'll write a scenario for the skit and prepare a final draft for day three. Keep in mind that scenarios are always written in present tense and have no dialogue, characterizations or details.

Day Three:

You and your parent will study your scenario, and together, write one which you'll use to write the script for a skit. You may use this small bit of a scenario as a model. Notice that the scenario is in present tense. You should use a place you know well.

Scenario
for
"At Dinner"

Bill is eating dinner with his middle class family in their suburban home. Bill's sister is seated across from him and his father is at the end of the table, on Bill's right, across from Bill's mother.
 Bill's father is asking Bill why he hasn't raked the leaves from the front lawn yet. Bill plays with his silverware. The rest of the family sits quietly.

When you've finished the scenario, make a list of the body movements for each character. Set your paper up to be like the following example: This means, unless your parents tell you otherwise, don't write in this book. Use your own paper and leave this book clean for your little brother or sister.

BODY MOVEMENTS

Character One (teen):

_____

_____

_____

_____

_____

Character Two (adult):

_____

_____

_____

_____

When your scenario and list of body movements are written and before you start writing your skit, you should ask your parent to look over your work.

Preparation:
You should start on the introduction to your skit.

This brief model skit may help. I suggest you have a narrative voice which uses **past tense, third person,** is **objective**, and is **non-involved**. If these are new terms or you have forgotten, look ahead at exercise #5, "Point of View."

At Dinner

Bill was eating dinner with his family. Bill's father, a large but soft-spoken man, had asked Bill why the front yard hadn't been raked yet. Bill was running his fork around his plate as if it were a hockey stick and the last pea were a puck.

"There has to be a good reason; you've had plenty of time," Mr. Smith said, looking at his son. Two small pieces of meat made the goal, and Bill was racing toward it with the pea/puck. He could hear the crowd in the

stands yelling his name. "Well, what about it, Bill?"

Mr. Smith's hands were lying flat on the tablecloth, one on either side of his plate.

The rest of the family was still, waiting for Bill's answer. Bill's mother was watching her husband, and Janet was staring at her plate, glad she wasn't in this conversation.

"I guess I forgot." Bill faked out the last guard and cut in toward the goal, the puck riding on the tine of his fork.

"Forgot? How could this be, Bill? I've reminded you of this little job three times this week. I'm not sure you're remembering your responsibilities as a member of this family. We all have to work together. Do you remember the times we've talked about that? How each of us has a job to help all of us?" Bill's father had raised his right hand in a questioning gesture. He looked at his wife.

Bill slapped a high shot right past the goalie's shoulder and the pea hit his father's coffee cup. "Sorry, Dad." Bill reached out and tried to spear the pea, but it rolled away from his fork. His other hand was inching toward his spoon. If he could just trap that Green Guz between the trident and his net, then he might be able to save the planet Oorf from the revenge of the Guz.

"About what?"

"What?"

Bill looked up at his father and saw for the first time that his expression was very intense, and Bill knew he had to shape up. He raked the pea toward his plate while he said, "How about I start tomorrow right after I get done with studies?"

Bill's father smiled at his wife and began to eat again. Bill had found a small piece of skin at the edge of his thumb that he wasn't sure he had ever seen before. He reached out for the scalpel and felt his nurse slap it into his palm. The patient was out and it was time to cut.

Days Four and Five:

You and your parent should work together on the skit. When you've finished, you might want to make a copy at the library so you won't have to write it twice.

PART THREE: Acting

Preparation:

You and your parent may want to memorize and produce the skit for the rest of your family. The skit should take between one and a half and two minutes to "play."

Day Six:

Arrange the furniture and invite the family to watch your skit. Don't worry about making mistakes. No one will know if you miss a word or skip a gesture.

The important thing is that you have a good time learning that people move their bodies with the ways their minds work.

I recommend you take the next week off from writing and spend the time reading and discussing ideas with your parents.

PROGRESS REPORT

Name:_____ Date:_____

Assignment #1: WHAT OUR FEET DO

Copy your best sentence for the week on the lines below.

_____

_____

Name one mistake you made this week that you can fix and will avoid next week.

_____

_____

Write the sentence that had this mistake in it.

_____

_____

Write the sentence again showing how you fixed this mistake.

_____

_____

Comments:

#2 IF I WERE A . . .

Skill Strand: Research and Report

It may take you eight days to learn that:
1. The things we call good and bad (our attitudes) are determined by who we are
2. Some ideas may be looked at in more than one way
3. The organization of a report should help the reader understand it

PREWRITING

Day One:

All people don't have the same attitudes. This doesn't mean that if you don't like the same things I do, I think you're bad. People can disagree and still share respect.

These kinds of attitudes, about what is considered good, are reasonable and expected because the things we call good and bad are determined by who we are and what experiences we've had. People who have had different experiences should have different feelings. It wouldn't be right, with the experiences I've had, for me to try to impose my attitudes on you because you wouldn't understand or appreciate them.

In this exercise you'll have a chance to look at two attitudes and explain that both, though they're opposite, are good for the people holding (believing) them.

Most middle class Americans feel very protective about their property. Land they have bought and live on is precious to them, and they like to mark it off as theirs and in many cases put up fences around it. Many people even have arguments about who owns small strips of land that lie between their properties.

A strange situation developed when the settlers came to this land. Many of the tribes of Indians living here had attitudes about the land that were not understood by the settlers. They felt that people couldn't own land; it was just there. The land belonged to the world or the Great Spirits and men couldn't possess it. Men could live on the land and use it, but the land would always be there. When they died, someone else would use it.

The settlers believed that it was valuable to own land. This created problems. Here were people living on land who knew that men couldn't own land, and along came a group of people who wanted to "buy" the land; actually give them wonderful things for it.

At first, many of the Indians thought this was funny—people giving them beautiful knives, beads and mirrors for something that no one could own. In this way what is now Manhattan Island was "bought" by the Dutch settlers for less than thirty dollars worth of trinkets. The Indians thought they had gotten a great bargain.

The people from Europe, of course, felt they had made a wonderful buy. The first trouble began between the Indians and the settlers when the settlers wanted the Indians to keep off of the property they had just purchased.

In this exercise you're going to pretend that you're a lawyer who has to explain these different attitudes toward land to members of the Continental Congress who will have to make treaties with the Indians.

What you've been hired to do is to make clear the two differing attitudes which have to do with owning land. This information you'll have to make up. You'll have to invent the examples (cases) you'll use.

You must make the Congressmen understand that there are two real sets of attitudes in conflict. Your job is to explain this so that both sides are treated fairly—so that the Indians are not taken advantage of and the settlers can own the land they have bought. You're not to come to any decisions for the lawmakers. **This is not a court case.** You've only to **explain** the two attitudes and how they are in conflict.

WRITING

In this paper you must explain the history of land use as it's seen by both the settlers and the Indians. The congressmen must understand this before they can understand how the two groups feel.

This will be hard to do. You'll have to invent the history of the Indians' use of land and how they feel about selling it. You'll have to give examples (cases) where the Indians dealt with land use before the white men came.

> *Think about bears using the land. How the bears don't own the land except where their feet are making prints. And, when they move, their land changes to where their feet make new prints.*

9

I just made this up. But, this is an example of how you can make up material for this report. It would be better if you could research this topic, but that would be hard if you don't have a library handy. Your parent may want to encourage you to research this in your local library. If you have an historical society in your town, some member should be happy to help you. Or, If you were to follow this outline, it might help you organize your paper:

1. An **introduction** to your report to the lawmakers which could contain:

    A. Who you are
    B. What you want to do
    C. Why you want to do this
    D. How the information you'll give them will help them make the decisions they'll have to make.

2. A **history** of the Indians' use of land and their philosophy about land ownership.

    A. "**Cases**," which you'll make up, which will serve as examples of how the Indians' attitudes control their beliefs and behaviors.
    B. A **request** from the Indians that the Congressmen respect their values.

3. A **history** of the settlers' use of land and their philosophy about land ownership.

    A. "**Cases**," which you'll make up, which will serve as examples of how the settlers' attitudes control their beliefs and behaviors.
    B. A **request** from the Settlers that the Congressmen respect their values.

4. A **conclusion** to your report that explains to the Congressmen how both attitudes concerning land use and ownership are good systems and have worked for the people involved.

    A. An **appeal** to the Congressmen that they take into consideration the Indians' attitudes.
    B. An **appeal** to the Congressmen that they take the attitudes of the Settlers into account.
    C. A **statement of appreciation** for the opportunity to present this report to the Congress.

This organization might be easier to understand with an outline of the parts of this paper:

This paper is a report and its title should let your reader know this. It could look like the example on the next page.

REPORT ON THE PROBLEMS
of
DIFFERING ATTITUDES
CONCERNING
USE AND OWNERSHIP OF LAND
PRESENTED
to the
CONTINENTAL CONGRESS
1776

Your paper should be set up to be like the example page below:

(Your first and last name)

(The date)

(Skip two spaces)

(The Title Of Your Paper)

(Skip one line)

INTRODUCTION (Don't label the parts of your paper like **INTRO or**
BODY)

   1 Who you are

   2 What you want to do

   3 Why you want to do this

   4 How this information will help

BODY   (Skip _no_ lines)

   1 Indians' use of land and philosophy

   2 "Cases," examples of Indians' attitudes

   3 Request Congressmen respect the Indians' beliefs

                                          (Skip _no_ lines)

   1 Settlers' use of land and philosophy

   2 "Cases," examples of settlers' attitudes

   3 Request Congressmen respect the settlers' beliefs

CONCLUSION   (No labels)

   1 An appeal for Congress to consider the Indians' attitudes

   2 An appeal for Congress to consider the settlers' attitudes

   3 Appreciation for opportunity to present this report

(Equal margins on all side of each page and page #s on all but page #1)

Of course, you're not to use my example title. This is just an example. Your introduction could be structured to be like the outline below. You should **not use second** person.

The legal firm of Bean, Bean and (your name) in presenting this report Congress has commissioned. . .

(1) *You are a representative of the Philadelphia law firm of Bean, Bean and_____?*
(2) *You are presenting a report that the Congress has commissioned the firm to do on the different attitudes that the contesting groups have regarding land use and ownership.*
(3) *Your firm has agreed to do this study because of the serious nature of the problem.*
(4) *There have been numerous killings over ownership of land. The firm of Bean, Bean,_____hopes that their report will help the Congressmen understand both sides in this controversy and the various attitudes held by the contestants.*

In this example I used just one sentence for each of the points in the introduction. You may use as many as you need or like.

Day Two:
You'll have to decide how you're going to describe the second point, the history of the Indians' land use and their attitudes concerning land ownership. You should make up a "case" to use as an example. It might be like the example case below:

> *Honorable Congressmen, an example of how the Indians feel about land ownership can best be shown by this strange but touching story about the Indians and their land.*
>
> *There was, on a river not far from here, a small tribe of Indians called the Timawut. They had a patch of ground they used for growing maize. A family of beavers moved onto their land and built a dam across their small river. The water rose higher every day. When it was almost to their maize field, one of the nearby settlers asked the Indians why they did not tear down the dam and save their food. They replied that the beaver had as much right to the land as they did. It would anger the great spirits if they were to destroy the home of the beavers.*
>
> *The Indians moved their maize field to higher ground. The following year there was very little rain. The river all but dried up, but the lake the beavers had made with their dam held enough water so that the Indians could water their crops.*
>
> *The Indians and animals have lived together in harmony for thousands of years.*

Preparation:
You should show your parent for day three what you've written of the rough draft of point two.

Day Three:
After you've looked over the rough draft of point two, you should ask your parent to read your work. After you've been given suggestions for improving your writing, you should continue working on point two.

You should plan how you'll get a rough draft of point two written by day four.

Preparation:
Bring in on day four the rough draft of point two.

Day Four:
Make sure your parent reads the rough draft of point two at the beginning of your session today. You should begin working on point three.

This part should be much easier for you to write than was the second point. The settlers' attitudes concerning land use and ownership would have been much like ours are today. Make up a case that will show how the settlers' attitudes determine how they think about land.

Preparation:
You should write the second rough draft of point two and then finish the first rough draft of the third point.

Day Five:
Ask your parent to read your second rough draft of point two and your first rough draft of point three. Plan the conclusion to your report.

Preparation:
Write the final copy of the introduction and point two. You can write the second rough draft of point three.

Day Six:
Have your parent read your second draft of point three. You can finish writing the conclusion.

Preparation:
Write the final copy of point three and the rest of the rough draft of the conclusion.

Day Seven:

After your parent has had a chance to look over the first draft, you can work on the second draft of the conclusion. You'll have to write the final copy of the conclusion.

Preparation:

Bring in your finished paper for day eight.

Day Eight:

Your parent may want some member of your family to read the report as if it were being read to the Congress in 1776.

I recommend you take the next week off from writing.

PROGRESS REPORT

Name:_____ Date:_____

Exercise #2: IF I WERE A. . .

Copy your best paragraph for the week on the lines below.   (Read that again)

_____

_____

_____

_____

_____

Name one mistake you made this week that you can fix and will avoid next week.

_____

Write the sentence that had this mistake in it.

_____

_____

Write the sentence again showing how you fixed this mistake.

_____

_____

Comment:

#3 DESCRIBING CHARACTERS

Skill Strand: Creative

It may take you four days to learn that:
1. Authors have choices of what they describe
2. These choices are made to give their readers the information they want them to have
3. You can select what you describe to give your readers the information you want them to have

PREWRITING

Day One:

Authors create the world their characters live in. Before they begin writing, there are no people exactly like the ones they create, and there are no places just like the ones they put their people in.

When authors want to show their readers what characters are like, they first decide what the characters' major characteristics are and then create situations so the readers will see those characteristics.

This means that writers must pick a few things about their characters that they feel are important and let their readers understand them. They then will represent each whole character, and the readers will know the characters from what the writers chose to write about. If this is not clear, it will be in a moment.

One of the rules of writing fiction is that authors don't tell their readers what they want them to know, they show them what they want them to know. If we were to create a character and want to have our reader not like him because he doesn't ever think about other people, we would *not* tell our reader directly what the character is like. We would not say: *Groton didn't like other people and showed this by the way he acted towards them. He didn't wash and used bad table manners.*

Instead, we would have to show our reader how Groton acts and let our reader come to the conclusion that Groton doesn't like other people. It might read like this short example on the next page:

16

Most of the women were in the kitchen, wiping their hands on dish towels. The men were in the living room watching the ball game. The kids, all twelve of them, were moving from room to room getting in the way.

Dinner was on hold. My Aunt Edna asked Mom if Groton had been told when to come. The older kids were snatching bits of turkey as they walked past the platter.

The talk died as the family began to get tense with waiting. Mom whispered, "I don't know how long I can keep the stuffing hot without overcooking it."

Ripples of excitement came from the front of the house, and I knew that Groton had arrived. I ran to the front window, and there across the street was the rusty pick-up truck I remembered from last year.

Groton pushed his way to the end of the table and put his hands on the back of the large chair usually held for Dad. It looked like he had rubber gloves on. I had never seen his hands so clean.

Mom called the men to the table, and by the time they had shuffled to the dining room, Groton was sitting down and pulling up the sleeves of his flannel shirt, and now everyone could see his dark arms ending in the unnaturally white hands.

There was a shifting of kids away from Groton's end of the table, and I could smell, over the rich turkey and stuffing. . .

In this example I don't tell you that Groton doesn't care what other people think. But, you know this is true by the description of his actions and his family's reaction to him.

WRITING

You're to write about a character, but first you should decide what one characteristic would best show that character's personality. Then you'll have to create a place where the reader can watch this character operate.

The four steps to this exercise are:

1. Decide on one characteristic for a character. It could be something like:
   A) Stingy
   B) Scared or frightened of life
   C) Greedy
   D) Kind
   E) Empathetic

2. Decide what you'll describe about this character.
   (This can be actions, physical characteristics or both.)

3. Put your character in a place. (This should be where the characteristic can be observed by your reader.)

4. Write a short description (less than 600 words) of an event in which your reader will see your character operate and will understand what kind of a person your character is.

Preparation:
Prepare for day two, the name of your character, your character's major characteristic, and the place and event about which you'll write. Your preparation (it's hard not to prepare when you work at home, isn't it?), might look like this:

1. Name of character: Janet

2. Major characteristic: Janet is very shy. This characteristic will be shown to my reader by my showing Janet when she will not talk or look at another person.

3. I plan on showing Janet's shyness by describing a time in a Burger King restaurant when Janet and her girlfriend run into two boys they had met at their youth group.

Day Two:
Write the first draft of your description. If you didn't get your preparation done for today, be sure and let your parent know so you can get the help you need.

Preparation:
Work over your rough draft and then rewrite it. It's always possible, especially for young writers, to cut extra words and clean up rough drafts. See the example at the end of this exercise.

Day Three:
Make sure your parent reads your second draft as soon as possible. (Do this.)

Preparation:
Write your **final rough draft**. This means that you've cut out all the parts that don't need to be there, you've changed all of the rough sentences into smooth ones, and you've checked the punctuation and spelling.

Day Four:
As soon as your parent has read your final rough draft, begin the **final copy**. By now your parent should have had a chance to read your work three or four times. If this is not the case you're either not working hard enough or you're not making sure you're getting the help you need.(Correct this situation.)

Preparation:
Your final draft will be due at the start of day five.

EXAMPLE:

To show you that everyone's work can be cut and made better, I've included my first and second drafts of the beginning of my description of Groton. Notice how the piece gets shorter, but the cutting of parts of it doesn't hurt it but helps it by making it "cleaner."

1st draft

Everyone, all the relatives we could squeeze into our house but Groton, had come. Most of the women were in the kitchen, "helping." The men were in the living room watching the ball game on the television. The kids, all twelve of them, were running and yelling and chasing each other from room to room getting in everyone's way.

The dinner was on "hold." Some of the women were asking if Groton had been told when to come, and the older kids were snitching bits of turkey and even taking some choice bits into the men in the living room.

2nd draft

Everyone but Groton had come. Most of the women were in the kitchen "helping." The men were in the living room watching the ball game on the TV. The kids, all twelve of them, were moving from room to room getting in everyone's way.

The dinner was on "hold." Some of the women were asking if Groton had been told when to come and the older kids were snitching bits of turkey when they walked past the platter.

3rd draft

Most of the women were in the kitchen, wiping their hands on dishtowels. The men were in the living room watching the ball game. The kids, all twelve of them, were moving from room to room getting in the way.

Dinner was on hold. The older kids were snatching bits of turkey as they walked past the platter. My Aunt Edna asked Mom if Groton had been told when to come.

I recommend you take the next week off from writing.

PROGRESS REPORT

Name:_____ Date:_____

Exercise #3: DESCRIBING CHARACTERS

Copy your best sentence for the week on the lines below.

_____

_____

Name one mistake you made this week that you can fix and will avoid next week.

_____

_____

Write the sentence that had this mistake in it.

_____

_____

Write the sentence again showing how you fixed this mistake.

_____

_____

Comments:

#4 CONFLICT

Skill Strand: Creative

It may take you seven days to learn that:
1. Conflicts are an important part of fiction and they are resolvable
2. You can create and resolve conflicts in your writing

PREWRITING

Day One:

Every story you've ever read has been based on a conflict, because this is what a story is, an incident in which a conflict is resolved. In this exercise you'll have a chance to write about conflict and its resolution (ending).

This exercise has **5 parts**. You will:

1. **Write a scenario**   4. **Put the characters in conflict**
2. **Create characters**   5. **Resolve the conflict**
3. **Describe a scene**

WRITING

A scenario is an outline in sentence and paragraph form of a story or an event. It has **characters, situation and a series of events**, but it has **no details or dialogue**. It's the **skeleton** upon which a story is based.

You must write a scenario for a very short story in which two characters are in conflict. Some examples may help you select a situation:

1. A boy doesn't want to clean his bedroom because it will make him late for his ball game. His mother won't let him leave the house until this is done. How is this conflict resolved?

2. A neighbor claims that Mr. Smith's son has been riding his bike across his lawn. Mr. Smith claims that the neighbor's dog has been making a mess of his yard. How do these two neighbors solve this conflict?

3. Sisters would like to wear the same sweater to the party. They both can't wear it and this causes a conflict. How can this be resolved?

4. A girl, who is two years younger than her older sister, doesn't get as good grades as her sister. Her mother is careful not to compare the progress of the two girls, but she can see that there is some resentment in her younger daughter toward her sister. How can the mother solve the coming conflicts between the two girls?

5. A teenager, either a boy or girl, wants a Moped, a small motor scooter, and mom thinks her child is too young. What happens and why?

6. Mr. Jones thinks that some money is missing from the cash register. Since Janet is the only young person working in the store, and all of the other people who work there have been there a long time, he feels that Janet may have been helping herself. He suggests that Janet pay back the twenty dollars that is missing. Janet didn't take the money and doesn't feel she should pay it back. How is this conflict resolved?

A scenario can read like this example of the start of a scenario (note the tense):

> *John is one of two pitchers on the church softball team. This weekend will be the playoff where the championship will be decided. The team is counting on John because their other pitcher has hurt his arm. If John doesn't play, the team won't stand a chance, and all the members of the team have worked really hard this year, because the church team has never won a championship, and they finally might.*
>
> *John's father calls on Thursday and says he can come home for the weekend. He has been away on business for the last two months setting up the new office in California. On Monday he will have to go back. He asks John if he would like to go on a short fishing trip with him.*

(Did you note the tense? If not, why not?)

Preparation:
Prepare for day two the finished rough draft of your scenario.

Day Two:
While your parent reads your scenario, you should begin writing your conflict. After your parent has made suggestions, you can write the final copy. When you start your conflict, the first thing you'll have to do is select your point of view. Remember, you'll have to create and maintain a narrative voice. I'd recommend third person and past tense. You'll have to decide on the rest of the options yourself.

Your narrative voice decisions should be listed at the top of the page. You might refer to the next exercise in this book that describes narrative voice point of view options.

(Don't use this example but your paper should be set up just as this example is.):

Point of View:

Tense: Past
Person: Third, singular
Attitude: Subjective
Knowledge: Limited to person
Perspective: Limited to person
Involvement: Part of action

You'll have to introduce your reader to your characters, place them in a location and start the conflict. A few suggestions might help you to get started:

CHARACTERS:

It will be easier for you to create believable characters if you make them like people you know. You'll then understand some of the motivations they might have. You could even copy their speech patterns. But, it might be good if you were to avoid using real names.

Note that people move and talk differently when they're upset than they do when they're not. You can show your characters' feelings by the things you have them do. In the scenario I gave you as an example, the conflict is an internal one—it is in John and centers on his sense of duty to his team and his desire to be with his father. It would be easier for you to create an external conflict—one between two people. Look at this short example developed from my scenario:

> *John put his glove and shoes in the hall closet and went to the basement to shower and wash his uniform. He was thinking about the Kings' lineup. He had watched many of their games and he was sure that he knew which players were suckers for his slow curve, and which ones he had to watch out for on his fast ball. If he were to do everything just right Saturday afternoon, his team could take the championship. The guys were counting on him and he had promised them that he would give it his best. After putting his uniform in the washing machine, he started the shower going.*
>
> *It was then that he heard the phone. He picked up the extension. It was his father. "Hi, Dad. When are you coming home? Mom said it might be this weekend. It that true?"*
>
> *"Sure is, John. I have a flight Friday morning and will be home by two o'clock. I got a surprise for you. How would you like to go on a short fishing trip with your mother and me? It's all arranged. We have a cabin on a terrific trout stream all rented. This is your birthday surprise. What do*

23

you say? Great, huh?"
       John said, "Sure is, Dad. Where's the cabin?" and then he realized
that he was committed this weekend to the game on Saturday.

LOCATION:

You know, of course, that people act differently in different places. You'll have to set your characters in a place before you can decide how to have them act.

It will be easiest for you to create places with which you're familiar. It would be hard for me to create a European palace scene because I've never been in such a place. But, it would be easy for me to create a classroom in a school.

CONFLICT:

The same rules apply for conflict that I gave you for character and location. You should write about some conflict with which you're familiar. It will be easier for you to write, and it will be easier for your readers to believe what you write.

It would be hard, or even impossible, for you to write about a conflict between two officers in the Air Force who are arguing about the flight characteristics of a new plane. The reasons for this are obvious. Apply this reasoning to your work and write about a conflict you understand.

Day Three:

You should plan for day three a rough draft of the start of your conflict piece. There should be an introduction of the place and characters. Ask your parent to read what you have and work during this session on the suggestions.

Preparation:

Rewrite what you have, using your parent's suggestions, and prepare for day four a rough drafting of the introduction to the conflict situation.

Days Four and Five:

You should be able to finish the rough draft of your piece by day five. You should have at least three or four pages of hand-written work by then. It should be about 800 words. Make sure your parent reads your work each day. You'll want to ask your parent if the motivation of your characters is clear.

Day Six:

Spend this time checking punctuation in your dialogue. Have your parent check that you've done it correctly.

Day Seven:

Your final draft should be done at the end of this session. Make sure it has a title and that your point of view choices are listed at the top of the first page. Format the top of your first page to be like this example page:

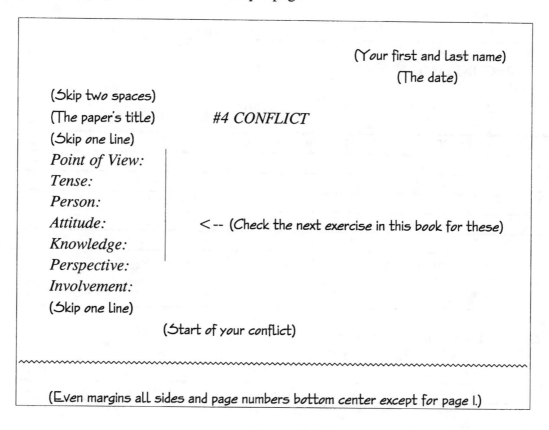

I recommend that you take a week off from writing.

PROGRESS REPORT

Name:_____ Date:_____

Exercise #4: CONFLICT

Copy your best paragraph for the week on the lines below.

_____
_____
_____
_____
_____
_____

Name one mistake you made this week that you can fix and will avoid next week.

_____

Write the sentence that had this mistake in it.

_____
_____

Write the sentence again showing how you fixed this mistake.

_____
_____

Comments:

#5 POINT OF VIEW

Skill Strand: Expository

It may take you six days to learn:
1. The choices an author has in his use of points of view
2. How these points of view elements work
3. That you can recognize points of view
4. The structuring of an explanatory exposition
5. To write an explanatory exposition

PREWRITING

Day One:

Any author's choice in the characteristics of narrative voice becomes part of that writer's style. Below is a listing of the major options (choices) an author has for narrative voice.

<table>
<tr><td colspan="3" align="center">NARRATIVE VOICE
POINT OF VIEW OPTIONS</td></tr>
<tr><td>PERSON:</td><td>first</td><td>third</td></tr>
<tr><td>NUMBER:</td><td>singular</td><td>plural</td></tr>
<tr><td>TENSE:</td><td>past   present</td><td>future</td></tr>
<tr><td>ATTITUDE:</td><td>objective</td><td>subjective</td></tr>
<tr><td>INVOLVEMENT:</td><td>part of action</td><td>observer</td></tr>
<tr><td>KNOWLEDGE:</td><td>limited omniscience
or
restricted to participation</td><td>restricted
to observation</td></tr>
<tr><td>PERSPECTIVE:</td><td>omnipresent overview</td><td>restricted to
personal view</td></tr>
</table>

PERSON and NUMBER

First Singular: The narrative voice, in its capacity as story teller, refers to itself as an individual and not part of a group, and uses *I*.

First Plural: The narrative voice, although speaking to the reader as an individual, constantly refers to itself as part of a group, and uses *we*.

Third Singular: The narrative voice refers to one character at a time and talks about groups of people only in the sense of them being observed by one individual: *He saw the boy,* or, *She saw the mayor in the garage.*

Third Plural: The narrative voice refers to a group of two or more people, using *they* or *them* as in *They saw the boy*.

TENSE

Past: The narrative voice talks about things that have already happened.

Present: The narrative voice refers to actions as if they were happening at the time of the telling about them.

Future: The narrative voice tells about things that will happen.

ATTITUDE

Objective: This voice shows no emotional involvement in the actions in the narration. The voice seems to have no attitude about the characters or what they do and assumes almost a scientific objectivity about the events.

Subjective: The narrative voice cares about the characters and what they do and lets the reader know this by making comments indicating it has made value judgments.

INVOLVEMENT

Part of action: The narrative voice is one of the characters who takes part in the events in either a main or supporting role.

KNOWLEDGE

Limited
omniscient: The narrative voice has a wide range of possibilities. It can be in more than one mind and can know what is happening in many places.

Restricted to: This voice has a fairly narrow view of events, as if it were speaking
observation from knowledge gained by looking out of a window watching the action in the house next door.

Restricted to This narrative voice is from someone who is part of the action and can't
participation: know what is happening in other places, nor can this voice know what happens to other characters when not with them.

PERSPECTIVE

Omnipresent The narrative voice must have some form of omniscience (knows
overview: everything), for it can describe things that take place in two locations at the same time. It can take readers into the past and future and can show them the actions from any angle or from any vantage point

Restricted to The narrative voice assumes the position of a character in the story,
personal view: either as a participant or as an observer. This view, then, is limited to what the voice can see and hear, as a normal person/character would be able to see and hear.

The following are examples of the use of these major elements of point of view:

PERSON: First and third, singular and plural:

First person singular: *I saw the dog.*
Third person singular: *He saw the dog.*
First person plural: *We saw the dog.*
Third person plural: *They saw the dog.*

TENSE: Past, present, future:

First person singular, past: *I saw the dog.*
Third person plural, past: *They saw the dog.*
First person singular, present: *I see the dog.*
Third person plural, present: *They see the dog.*
First person singular, future: *I will see the dog.*
Third person plural, future: *They will see the dog.*

ATTITUDE: Objective and subjective:

First person singular, past, objective: *I saw the hungry dog.*
Third person plural, future, subjective: *They will see the poor, hungry dog.*

INVOLVEMENT: Part of action, central or peripheral, observer (minimal or non-involved)

First person singular, past, subjective, central to action: *I felt sorry for the poor, hungry dog when I had to chase it away from the door.*

Third person singular, past, objective, non-involved: *He watched the cook chase the hungry dog away from the kitchen doorway.*

First person plural, past, subjective, minimally involved: *We held the door so the cook could chase away the poor dog.*

KNOWLEDGE: Limited omniscient, restricted to participation, restricted to observation:

Third person past, subjective, non-involved, observer, limited omniscient: *It was a cruel thing that the boys should have to hold the door when they felt so sorry for the lonely and hungry dog which the cook, who really hated all animals, chased away from the back of the trash-filled alley.*

First person singular, present, objective, minimally involved, knowledge restricted to action: *Opening the door for the cook, I can see the hungry dog and watch through the crack in the hinge-line as the cook throws a rock and chases it away.*

First person plural, past, subjective, non-involved, knowledge restricted to observation: *From our room over the alley we looked down on the back of the restaurant and there saw the two boys hold the door for the cruel cook so he could throw stones at the poor dog.*

PERSPECTIVE: Omnipresent overview, limited to personal view:

Third person past, objective, non-involved, limited omniscient, omnipresent overview: *The dog had been in the alley happily rooting in the garbage only a short time when the two not-very-bright boys opened the door, and the cook, who never had liked dogs, threw stones, and the frightened dog ran down to the corner and into the alley in the next block, where it found better pickings anyway.*

First person plural, present, objective, restricted to observation, knowledge limited to personal view: *By leaning over the sill and looking down we can see the door opening and someone throwing stones, and then the door shuts and the alley is empty again.*

STRUCTURE
for
EXPOSITORY ESSAYS

INTRODUCTION (has **three parts** in **one paragraph**): (*Read that again*)

1. **Background:**

This is information that the reader will find necessary to understand the contention (thesis statement). This can be a history of the subject or some personal experience and/or observation. (*Such as research, or a field trip of some kind*)

2. **Contention:**

This is a one-sentence statement of position or belief. This is what some people call the thesis statement—the point of the paper, and it is what the body will show to be true or valid.

3. **Process:**

Usually, this is a one-sentence statement indicating the order in which the body parts will support the contention. As exposition is essentially statement and support, everything in the body must be related to the contention in a supportive way and must appear in the same order as indicated in this process sentence.

This process sentence will have *key* words that will key the reader in to the ideas in the body in the order they will be presented. The key words will come from a breakdown of the contending idea. If the paper were to be about a new landfill proposal, the key words might be based on the ideas of *ecology, taxes, neighbors, zoning laws,* and *needs.*

BODY: (has as many <u>sections</u> of **paragraphs** as there are key words in the process): (*All you have to do is count.*)

The body, which must support the contention, contains material presented in the **same order** as are the points (key words) in the process. This is so that the parts of the body—each of which may be composed of a number of paragraphs—will be recognized by the reader as supporting the contending idea in the introduced order. (*Just check the order*)

CONCLUSION: (has **three parts** in **one paragraph**): (Read that again.)

1. A **restatement of the contending idea** but not using the same words.

2. A **reintroduction of the organizational aspect** of the process but not using the key words which were used in the process in the introduction.

3. A **connection** made between the **background, contention** and **body.**

(There is a lot of new material in this exercise. If you first read the entire directions and then do the sections one at a time, it should all come together. If you read the whole thing and then feel you don't understand it, that's okay. Just go back and do one part at a time. It'll work.)

THIS ORGANIZATION
APPLIED TO THIS EXERCISE

INTRODUCTION: (Read this carefully. You'll use it for years.)

1. **Background:** This material should explain the function of storytellers and the idea of the narrative voice, and that storytellers have choices of how they tell their stories.

2. **Contention:** The main idea of this paper should be that the choices of point of view are **not hard to understand or recognize.**

3. **Process:** the organization of this paper should be based on the choices that an author has in selecting the point of view. The process is a **one-sentence statement** showing the organization of the supportive material in the body of the paper. It should **contain the key words** that will be the points in the body.

   The key words that you're to use in the process sentence are the points of view choices: *PERSON,   NUMBER,   TENSE,   ATTITUDE,   INVOLVEMENT, KNOWLEDGE,* and *PERSPECTIVE.*   (Read this sentence again.)

   This means that you'll have to create a sentence with the key words in it in list form. It can be structured like the following sentence. *Most of the time at the picnic, I was with John, Bill, Janet, Jack and Betty.*   (A picnic and these kids will not be in this paper.)

BODY:

The body of your paper will be **organized** on the basis of the **key words in the process** statement. This means that there will be at least one paragraph for each of the key words.   (Read this again.)

The **first key word** in your **process** statement will be *PERSON,* so the **first section** in the **body** will be about the point of view choice, *PERSON.*

In this section of your body you should explain **how** *person* **is used** by the author and the **choices the author has in selecting person** for the narrative voice, and give **examples** of that author's choice of person. Check again the chart showing the choices and the examples showing how each choice works.

You should **use examples** from short stories or novels to show your reader how all the different choices work. If you can't find examples in books you might **make them up.**

There will be **seven key words in your process statement,** so there will be seven sections to the body of your paper. **Each section will be structured in the same way.**

CONCLUSION:

1. **The contention restated** (remember not to use the same words that you used in the introduction.)

2. **The process restated** (remember not to use the key words). This is hard to do. Your restatement of the process could read like this: *An author has seven elements to choose from to make up the narrative voice.*

3. The **connection** between the body and the background.

In this kind of writing the bodies of papers support the backgrounds so that there is always a relationship between them.

The background of this paper tells the reader an author's choices, and the body of this paper explains the function of those choices an author has.

On the following page is a diagram of an explanatory essay. It might pay you to make a copy of it and put it in your notebook. You'd then be able to refer to it when you have to write your papers in college.

DIAGRAM OF AN EXPLANATORY ESSAY

INTRODUCTION
(three parts) -->

1. Background
2. Contention
3. Process

BODY --->

The body should have as
many sections of paragraphs as
there are key words in the process.

CONCLUSION
(three parts) -->

1. Restatement of contending idea
   (not same words)
2. Mention of organization
   (do not use the key words)
3. A connection made between the body
   and the background

WRITING

Work on the introduction. The first thing you should write is the contention—that statement which tells the reader the point of the paper. This will become the **second** part of your introduction. It could have something to do with the choices an author has when creating the narrative voice. Write it here or on your own paper:

Contention:

_____
_____
_____
_____

The next step should be the writing of the process. This is the **third** part of your introduction, and it will show your reader how the body of your paper will be organized. It will contain those seven key words:

1. _____
2. _____
3. _____

4. _____
5. _____
6. _____

34

Using these seven key words write **the one sentence** which will become your **process** sentence:

_____

_____

_____

_____

_____

Background:

This part of your introduction must present enough information to the readers so that they can understand the contention. This will be the **first** part of your introduction. In this paper you might talk about what it means to tell a story. Remember that the author is not the storyteller, it's the narrative voice which has been created by the author which tells the story. The author has to build the narrative voice from the parts available. In this exercise, those parts are the choices an author has of points of view. Write your background on other paper.

Preparation:
Rewrite your introduction.

Day Two:

If you're still having trouble with the introduction, make sure you ask your parent for help early in this session. You should write the first section of the body today. It should be about the author's choices of person for the narrative voice.

You should be able to find material in your reading or in the library as examples to support your points. There should be one example for each of the choices the author has for the voice. This means that you should find a sentence in which the narrative voice speaks in first person and one in which the voice speaks in third person. When you have this written make sure your parent checks your work.

Preparation:
Write the second point and rewrite the finished rough draft of the first point.

Day Three:

Ask your parent to read your second point today. You'll be writing the third point.

Write the fourth point, and the finished rough draft of the second and third points.

Day Four:

Ask your parent to read over your fourth point and the rewriting of the second and third points. You should write the fifth point.

Preparation:

You should write the sixth point, rewrite the fifth point, and begin writing the final draft.

Day Five:

You should write the rough draft of the conclusion.

Day Six:

The finished paper will be due at the start of the session on day seven.

I recommend you take the next week off from writing.

PROGRESS REPORT

Name:_____ Date:_____

Exercise #5: POINT OF VIEW

Copy your best paragraph for the week on the lines below.

_____

_____

_____

_____

_____

_____

_____

_____

Name one mistake you made this week that you can fix and will avoid next week.

_____

Write the sentence that had this mistake in it.

_____

_____

Write the sentence again showing how you fixed this mistake.

_____

_____

Comments:

#6 WHAT MAKES IT WHAT IT IS

Skill Strand: Creative

It may take you six days to learn to:
1. Determine, for your reader, the character of a place
2. Establish a reader's feelings about a place by a description of only a portion of it

PREWRITING

Day One:

When authors decide to describe a place, like a room, they cannot describe all of it. It would take up a whole book to talk about everything. They must select what they'll show to their readers.

They have to decide what is important and what can be left out. In making this decision, they must analyze the character of the place and select those parts of it that will give their readers the feelings about it they want them to have.

It will help you understand how an author might do this if you think about the public library in your town. Most libraries have about the same character. They have fairly large rooms filled with tables, chairs and shelves of books. There usually are some easy chairs near the racks of magazines. There is a counter where books must be checked out. Most libraries are air conditioned and are very quiet places.

If an author were to want to describe a library, he or she'd be very selective in choosing what to describe. As an example of how this works, let me show you two situations a writer might create that would determine what would be described about a library in each one..

Situation One: (Not the description, rather the situation of the description)

> *It is dark on a cold fall evening. Betty has been walking home from her job at the hospital. For the last three blocks she has been hearing footsteps behind her. They have sounded closer each block, but, each time she has looked back, the street and sidewalks have been empty. As she*

nears the steps of the library, she realizes the sound of the footsteps are right behind her.

Just as she turns onto the walk to the large front doors, she hears the steps running.

Description: (Not the situation, rather the description of the situation)

Our writer would want to describe the main room of the library in such a way as to give the reader the feeling that Betty would be safe if she could just get inside, that there is order in the civilization in which she lives.

The writer would want to describe the library, as seen by Betty through the large front windows, to show control and stability. Our writer would describe the warmth of the room, the people reading at the tables, students taking notes, and the well ordered shelves of books. The reader would see normal people doing normal things: people who have secure lives, people who are protected from the fears Betty has.

Situation Two:

If an author were writing an adventure novel, it might be important to give the reader an entirely different feeling about a library. In this book an international terrorist has placed a poison canister in one of the water reservoirs that feed the city. It is set to release its contents in just fifty-four minutes.

The hero has identified one of the terrorists and has finally caught up with him in the library. The only way he can save thousands of people from being poisoned is by convincing this man to tell him the location of the poison canister.

Description:

He must try to reason with the man and/or plead with him to save the innocent people of the city. When the hero walks into the library, the author must describe the room. In doing this, the author would want to make the meeting more suspenseful by making the hero's job more difficult.

The hero would have to whisper very quietly. The reader might see the librarian frown at the two men when they begin to talk. Other people could look up from their books and shush them.

The author would want the reasonableness of the institution of the library to contrast with the madness of the terrorist, but, at the same time, the reader should be impatient with the petty rules about talking which make it difficult for the hero to save all of these people. In this second case, the reader should see the library as a symbol of civilized behavior that gets in the way of really important work that must get done.

WRITING

You'll create a place and then describe it as an author might to produce an attitude or feeling you want your reader to have. You'll do this **three (3) times**. Each time you'll set the scene, as I did, to show your parent why you want your reader to have the feelings you're creating. Each of the **three times** you'll want your reader to have **different feeling.**

This outline may help you get started: (There will not be enough room in this example for you to fill in the blanks. You'll have to set up an outline on your own paper.)

First situation: _____

_____

Main character: _____
What character wants: _____
Place character is in: _____
Feelings author wants reader to have: _____
Character of place: _____

Major characteristics of place described: _____

_____

Preparation:
If you didn't get **the three outlines** done today, prepare them for day two.

Day Two:

You should have enough written about the situations the heroes of your narratives are in to show your parents. This should take between 100 and 200 words each. On the two examples I've given you, I used 120 words in the first situation explanation and 140 words in the second. Your descriptions of the places, of course, will be longer. I'd suggest 400 to 500 words each. You're to start your first situation and description of place. By the end of this session, your parent should have had a chance to read your outline and first situation.

Preparation:
Prepare the rough draft of your first description.

Day Three:

Work on the situation for the second piece, and, as soon as your parent has had a chance to look at your first description, you can begin a revision of it.

Preparation:

Prepare for day four a finished rough draft of your first description. This means that you've gone over it for spelling and grammatical errors and that it's a "clean" copy.

Day Four:

Make sure your parent looks at the finished rough draft of the first description. You should work on the first draft of the second description while you're waiting for advice on the first. The final copy of the first description will be due on day five.

Preparation:

Prepare for day five: 1) the final copy of the first description; 2) a completed first rough draft of the second description; and, 3) the situation of the third description.

Day Five:

Your parent will read and comment on the first and second descriptions.

Preparation:

Prepare for day six the final copy of the second description; and the rough draft of the third description.

Day Six:

Your parent will read the rough draft of your third description. The final copy of the third description will be due at the start of day seven.

I recommend you take the next week off from writing. (Unless you rushed through the writing. This is important, so if you did rush, you should go back and do the whole thing over again.)

PROGRESS REPORT

Name:_____ Date:_____

Exercise #6: WHAT MAKES IT WHAT IT IS

Copy your best paragraph for the week on the lines below.

_____
_____
_____
_____
_____
_____
_____
_____

Name one mistake you made this week that you can fix and will avoid next week.

_____
_____

Write the sentence that had this mistake in it.

_____
_____

Write the sentence again showing how you fixed this mistake.

_____
_____

Comments:

#7 SURVEY

Skill Strand: Research

It may take you six days to learn to:
1. Write unbiased questions
2. Select a representative sample of respondents for a survey
3. Conduct an oral survey and write the final report

PREWRITING

Days One and Two:
There will be **three parts** to this exercise:

1. Writing unbiased questions
2. Selecting a representative sample to question
3. Asking the questions and writing the final report

PART ONE:

Market research (finding out how people feel about products) is big business in this country. People who can do this are in demand because they know how to ask questions so as to get answers that represent how people really feel.

One of the biggest problems market researchers have is trying to write questions which are unbiased (don't sway the response of the person being asked the question). This will make sense if you think of the questions you ask every day. The words you use and the ways you use them indicate your bias and so bias the responses you get.

Your parent may ask some of the members in your family to ask questions and let the rest of the family try and guess what the bias is of the person asking each question. This means that the family members will have to think of questions and then decide what they would like the answers to be and then ask the questions in such ways that they're likely to get the answers they wish. This exercise will be about how to write questions that don't bias the person being asked. You're to write five questions that have to do with young people in some way. They should be about what kids would know.

This will be an **attitude** survey and **not one of knowledge**. You cannot bias what people know, only what they think or feel.

To give you an example of how a biased question can influence the answer of the person being asked, I'll give you two questions: the first one will be written so as to try and influence the answer, and the second one will be written in such a way that I am more likely to find out what the respondent really feels.

1. Do you feel that most teenagers would like to be more sophisticated and grown up rather than so awkward and clumsy as they are?

2. Do you think that most teenagers would like to be more mature than they now are?

WRITING

Your job will be to write your questions the second way, without bias. Your five questions should be *yes* or *no* questions. This way you'll be able to figure out the percentage of the answers which are *yes* or *no*.

This is very hard to do, and you should have your parent check each question as soon as you finish it. (Do this. It'll save you time.)

PART TWO:

Days Three and Four:

Surveys are given to a small percentage of any group so that the people giving them will have an idea about how the whole group population feels or thinks about something without having to ask for an opinion from every person in the entire group.

Political parties and manufacturing companies are two of the groups which hire companies to take surveys.

These survey companies have to be able to trust that the answers to the questions given by the representative group are typical of the kinds of answers that the larger group would give or the survey would not be of any value to them.

As an example of how this works, pretend you're working for a company which writes and gives surveys. If I were to come to you and want you to take a survey in my school to find out if the kids like one brand of pink soft drink more than another brand, you'd have to do one of two things: You'd have to ask all of the kids in the school who had drunk both soft drinks, or you'd have to ask a representative sample of the kids who drink soda pop.

A sample means that you'd have to select a small group of kids who would then represent all of the kids in the school. This is called a representative sample.

It wouldn't be fair to me (your customer) if you were to ask kids who drink only Glow Pink Pop any more than it would be fair if you were to ask kids who drink only other brands.

You'd have to select a sample of kids to ask which would fairly represent all the kids in the school. In this way I, your customer, would have some idea about how all the kids in my school might feel.

There are two ways to select representative samples:
1. Random selection
2. A cross section selection

In the first case, **random selection**, the survey-taker selects names at random from a list of all the people in the large group. Sometimes this is done by selecting every twentieth or every hundredth name from the phone book or the voting registry.

In the second case, **cross section**, the make-up of the large group is studied and a small percentage of each of the major elements of the large group are selected as respondents.

Your parent will help you understand how a selection might be made of a representative sample of kids from a group using the second method, cross section selection. In this example there would have to be selected ten kids:
1. From all grades
2. From both sexes
3. From all ethnic groups

The pollster would have to make a list of the **kinds of kids** who would be asked. The list of ten kids selected to respond to the survey questions might look like this:
1. 5 boys
2. 5 girls
3. An equal number of kids from each of the grades in the group (if there were three grades, three tenth graders, three eleventh graders, and four twelfth graders would have to be selected).
4. If there were an ethnic mix in the school, a selection of respondents would have to be in the same proportion as the mix in the school. This means that if half of the kids in the school were Latino, there would have to be five Latino respondents. In this way the sample would represent, in percentage, the whole school. Your parent can help you figure out this part for the group of kids you select.

Now the list could be made more detailed:

1. One Anglo boy - tenth grade
2. Two Latina girls - tenth grade
3. One Latino boy - eleventh grade
4. Two Anglo girls - eleventh grade
5. Two Anglo boys - twelfth grade
6. One Latina girl - twelfth grade
7. One Anglo boy - twelfth grade

You'll not decide on the particular people you'll ask the questions of. You'll decide only on the types of people you'll ask. This would be hard to do but you'd have to ask kids you don't know really well to get information you might be able to trust. If you were ask your best friends for the answers to your questions, they might make a joke out of the exercise.

If how to select the kids to ask is not clear to you, be sure and ask your parent for help in understanding it. (Ask only after you have read again this section and studied it.)

PART THREE:

Days Five and Six:

Of course, you may not have access to kids in a school. You'll have to pick a group of kids you can get to. This could be a 4H group, Boy or Girl Scouts, youth group, athletic team members, church choir, or any other group.

This survey should be oral. This means that you should read the questions to the respondents. You should not let the kids being asked read the questions, and you should not answer questions they might ask about the questions or the subject.

It will help you to have the questions written on the same page with the list of the kinds of kids who will answer them. There should be a place where you can write the answers. This paper might look like the example on the next page:

I've put the listing of the kinds of kids who will be respondents at the top of the page so that if you do this you could keep track of the kinds of kids you've asked and which kinds to ask next.

- One Anglo boy - tenth
- Two Latina girls - tenth
- One Latino boy - eleventh
- Two Angla girls - eleventh

- Two Anglo boys - twelfth
- One Latino girl - twelfth
- One Anglo boy - twelfth

1. Do you prefer pink soda pop to the other brands?

yes_____   no_____

Your parent will show you how to show answers by four vertical marks and one slash mark to represent five answers that are the same.

Your final paper should have an introduction to the section where you report the results of the survey. You might use the outlining below to help you.

INTRODUCTION:

The reader of your report needs to know the following things about the survey you took, and this means that this information should be at the top of the paper you turn in.

1. What the **point** of the survey was and **who requested** it
2. **Who took the survey** and **where** it was taken
3. What **method** was used to **select the respondents**
4. What **percentage** of the large group were asked (How many kids were asked and what percent that was of the total group population. If you ask ten kids and the group population is 300, you'd have to figure out the percentage from these two numbers. You might check your math book to see if it might show you how this is done.)
5. The **method of asking** the questions (oral)   (This information doesn't have to be in this order.)

BODY:

The body of your paper should contain the questions and the percentage of the respondents who answered in a positive way. It should look like this sample:

Thirty percent of the respondents indicated that they prefer Glow Pink Pop to the other brands.

Your final paper will not be an essay, but just the introduction and a compilation of the results

I recommend you take the next week off from writing.

PROGRESS REPORT

Name:_____ Date:_____

Exercise #7: SURVEY

Copy your best paragraph for the week on the lines below.

_____
_____
_____
_____
_____
_____
_____
_____

Name one mistake you made this week that you can fix and will avoid next week.

_____
_____

Write the sentence that had this mistake in it.

_____
_____

Write the sentence again showing how you fixed this mistake.

_____
_____

Comments:

#8 ARGUMENT

Skill Strand: Expository

It may take you six days to learn to:
1. Establish a position on a local, controversial issue
2. Interview local experts
3. Find support in the library for a position on the issue
4. Use quotations from experts to support your position
5. Write an argumentative exposition supporting your position

PREWRITING

Day One:

For the rest of your life people will expect you to support the positions you hold with evidence and not just with your prejudices. If you tell others that you believe something, they'll expect you to quote authorities on the subject. Authorities are people who are recognized by reputation or position as knowing more than the rest of us and are respected for their knowledge.

Authorities hold positions or have jobs such as: the president's National Security Advisor, the Surgeon General, the president of General Motors, the high school principal, the president of the local board of education or the leader of a church. The editors and editorial writers of major magazines and newspapers are also considered authorities and can be used to support your position.

This exercise has **five** steps:
1. **Select a topic** and a **position** on that topic
2. Find **authorities** on the topic
3. **Take statements** from experts supporting your position
4. Find support in the **library** for your position
5. Use **quotations** in a paper of argument for your position

STEP ONE: Select a Topic and Position

There must be lots of local issues that are controversial. These are things that people don't agree on. Some possibilities are:

- Young people in contact sports such as football
- The pressures of homeschooling
- Competition in sports
- Prayer in public school
- Teaching of evolution or creation science
- Peer group pressures
- Dangers in eating junk food
- Religious programs in public places such as Christmas scenes on public land
- Abortion
- Affirmative action
- Toxic waste disposal

Your first job today is to select a controversial subject and decide on a position.

This part of your paper should look similar to this example.

Bill Smith
English
Feb. 9

ARGUMENT

Subject: Contact sports for young athletes

Position: Against

STEP TWO: Find authorities on the subject

You're to use two sources as authorities for this paper:
1. **Local experts**
2. **Newspaper and magazine editors, editorial writers** and **articles** from newspapers and/or magazines

This will give you an opportunity to use both **primary** and **secondary** research.

PRIMARY:

This is material that others have not collected for you. This comes from newspapers from the period involved, interviews, original photographs, original letters, diaries and maps. Primary material is material you collect yourself. You must conduct the survey and record the results, or take the pictures yourself or collect pictures from the people who own them, or draw the maps, or find copies of the newspapers of the time if you're going to call it primary material.

SECONDARY:

This is material that others have collected, such as articles in magazines and newspapers, history or reference books, surveys and reports that have been published, and interviews that have been printed.

For the secondary material in support of your position, your parent will want you to go to the library. The librarian may show you where the supports for the positions can be found. When you support your position with secondary materials, you have to give your reader information about where the materials come from. You should **name** the source (magazine, book or newspaper), give the **date** of publication, the **publisher** and sometimes even the **page**.

This should be done even if you're not listing a bibliography. This information for this paper should be **included in the body** of the paper. This could look like this:

> *Doctor John R. Williams is reported to have said, according to <u>Time</u> magazine, in its June 15, 1999 issue, that junk food is better for teenagers than some other foods. <u>Time</u> reports that Dr. Williams' in his speech to the American Medical Convention audience in St. Louis, on March 23, 1999, stressed that ". . .junk food has more energy that can be used by teenagers than most balanced meals."*

The sources for your support should **not** be put in footnotes or in endnotes unless you're writing what is called a term paper or you're asked to do so for a specific exercise, and you should include a bibliography only if asked to do so.

There will be authorities in your area on any topic which deals with local matters. You're to list the authorities you plan on contacting for quotations to use in your paper. This list should be on the paper you turn in which identifies your argument.(See example on the next page.)

Your parents may want to approve of your interviews. This means that they might want to decide if you should interview certain people, for instance, the custodian in the park. It might be that your parents will want to be with you when you do some interviews.

The paper you give your parent for day one should now look like the one below:

Bill Smith
English
Feb. 9

ARGUMENT

Subject: Contact Sports for Young Athletes

Position: Against

Authorities: 1. Bill Butts, the coach of the little league soccer team
2. Dr. Wells, family doctor
3. Betty Fitters, the local high school health teacher
4. Mrs. Smith, the author's mother (All mothers are experts.)

Day Two:
WRITING

STEP THREE: Take quotations on the Subject

You're to write the questions you'll ask the authorities on your subject. (See the example below.)

These questions should be written so that the authorities can not answer with a *yes* or *no*. You should ask what are called open-ended questions.

A good interview question is built on an answer given by the interviewee. This means that the questions prepared in advance of the interview are general and they all may not be asked. Each one might be followed by three or four questions based on what the interviewee replies to a previous question.   (This takes practice.)

You can see how poor an interview the following would make:

Q: Mr. Smith, do you think the kids in the youth group should smoke?
A: No.
Q: Do you feel there should be a place off the church grounds where kids could smoke?

A: No.
Q: Do you think the store on the corner should be fined for selling cigarettes to kids?
A: Yes
Q: Do you see yourself as a role model for the kids?
A: Yes.

See below for an example of an interview.

Your parent will give back to you the paper you handed in on day one, and you'll add this information to it. Your paper then should look like this:

Bill Smith
English
Feb. 9

ARGUMENT

Subject: An atomic waste dump in our county.

Position: Against

Authorities: *1. Mrs. Good, the mayor*
                2. Betty Fish, the biology teacher from the local college
                3. Jane Wells, the public health director for the county
                4. Mr. Slope, the county drain commissioner

Questions for interviewees:

1. Why is it that some people feel that a low level atomic waste dump in our county would be good for us?
2. Why do you feel that a waste dump would or would not pollute the ground water even if the waste is active for thousands of years?
3. Which do you feel is more important in this decision, the few jobs that will be created or the possible health hazards for the residents of this county, and why do you feel that way?

Days Three and Four

Preparation:
Interview authorities on your list. A few suggestions on quoting your experts may help. It's not necessary to quote everything that is said. You can choose what you want to use, but you'll have to show your reader that this is what you're doing. This can be done in this manner: If your interviewee says, *I have been mayor in Elton for 12 years, and I have felt for years that there must be a way to create new jobs*, and you want to quote just the part about new jobs, you can use **ellipsis (just 3 dots . . .)** to show that part of what was said is left out. It could look like these two examples below.

1. *"I have felt. . .there should be a way to create new jobs."*

2. *". . .there should be a way to create new jobs."*

When you transcribe (write up) your interviews, they can look like this example (see outline of body below which corresponds to numbers in the above list of questions.):

(1)   Mrs. Sue Good, the mayor of Elton, was (2) in her office when she was asked for her views on the question of a nuclear waste dump. She was reading the fashion page of the local paper and put it down when I walked in.

Q: (3 & 4) Mrs. Good, What problems would you expect if there were to be a nuclear waste dump?

A: "That's a good question. I've . . .thought for years that we should have a way to create new jobs."

Q: What do you feel are the reasons we shouldn't have a dump in our county?

A: "There. . .are two reasons that I can think of. One is that many of the residents of the county don't want it, and nobody wants to go against the will of the people. And the second is the EPA [Environmental Protection Agency] hasn't given this dump its clearance yet."

(5)   Those are certainly two good reasons why we shouldn't have such a dump here in our county. Think what a problem we might have if all public officials felt this way but were to vote for the dump anyway.

STEPS FOUR AND FIVE: Use quotations and your research in an argumentative exposition

You're to start the writing of your paper during this session. This outline might help:

INTRODUCTION: (see example below)
1. History of controversy
2. Your position
3. A statement about why you've decided to support your position

BODY:
(Based on the interviews you had and the quotations you found in the library.)

1. Point number one
2. Point number two
3. Point number three

Each interview section of your body should be structured like this (see example on previous page):

1. Name of interviewee
2. Place of the interview
3. The questions asked of the interviewee
4. The quotations taken from the answers given by the interviewee
5. How this interview supports your position

Each quotation taken from a source in the library should be structured like this (see previous example):

1. Name of the person quoted
2. The person's position, title or authority to speak on the issue
3. The name, publisher and date of the magazine, book or newspaper from which the quotation was taken
4. How this quotation supports your position

CONCLUSION: (see example on next page)
Your position restated (don't use the exact words you used in the introduction)

Your **INTRODUCTION** can be set up to be like this example:

(1)   *Every few years someone in Elton County raises the need to bring new jobs into the county. Often this is in some way related to a waste dump or a landfill facility. Now the county commissioners have suggested a nuclear waste dump. Many of the citizens of the county are against this proposal as are the business manager, Mr. Books, the biology teacher at Elton Junior College, Dr. Fish, and Mrs. Good, the mayor of Elton City, the county seat.*

(2)   *This question has been raised again this year. I am against the county having such a dump. However there are a number of people in favor of this proposal and both sides of any controversy must be examined before any decision is justified. I have investigated this situation as well as I was able and feel for the good of the people in our county that I have to remain strong in opposition to this dump proposal.*

Your **CONCLUSION** can be set up to be like this example:

After interviewing a number of experts in the county and doing considerable research in the public library on the subject of atomic waste dumps, my views on the proposed dump site controversy remain the same. I am still against the county having a dump site of this nature.

DIAGRAM OF THIS PAPER

INTRODUCTION

(3 parts) ------------ >
1. History of controversy
2. Your position
3. Why you support it

BODY

(supported by
interviews ----------- >
and research)
1st point
2nd point
3rd point

CONCLUSION --- >   Position on controversy restated

Day Five:

You should have the introduction and the rough draft of most of the body done. Start the conclusion today.

Preparation:

Write the finished rough draft of the body. This means that you'll have checked your paper for mechanical and spelling errors. A finished rough draft is a "clean" copy. It doesn't have many cross-outs and write-overs.

Day Six:

Your final copy will be due at the start of day seven.

(This type of paper is work, but, if you go to college, you'll have to write many like it.)

I recommend you take the next week off from writing.

PROGRESS REPORT

Name:_____ Date:_____

Exercise #8: ARGUMENT

Copy your best paragraph for the week on the lines below.

_____
_____
_____
_____
_____
_____
_____
_____

Name one mistake you made this week that you can fix and will avoid next week.

_____
_____

Write the sentence that had this mistake in it.

_____
_____

Write the sentence again showing how you fixed this mistake.

_____
_____

Comments:

SPELLING LIST

Every time you or someone else finds a misspelled word in your papers, write it in the column below. This is not to give you a list of words to study; rather, it's a listing to let you know what your problems are. I'd suggest you pick one word a week that gives you trouble. One that you use a lot. Learn that word this week, and next week pick another word to learn. Watch for that word in all of your reading and writing. In this way, in two or three years, you'll have a good basic spelling vocabulary.

(Have your parents check the manual called *Evaluating Writing* for this process.)

_____

_____

_____

_____

_____

_____

_____

_____

_____

_____

_____

FIRST SEMESTER REPORT

WRITING SKILLS MASTERY

SEVENTH LEVEL WRITING EXERCISES

Student:_____   Date:_____

Exercise 1: What Our Feet Do
Skill Strand: Creative

Skill Mastered	Needs Experience	
____	____	1. Understanding that people vary in the ways they move their bodies.
____	____	2. Realizing that writers understand this and use it in their writing
____	____	3. Using this understanding in creating characters

Exercise 2: If I Were A . . .
Skill Strand: Research and Report

____	____	1. Understanding that the things we call good and bad (our attitudes) are determined by who we are
____	____	2. Accepting that ideas may be looked at in more than one way
____	____	3. Understanding that the organization of a report should help the reader understand it

Exercise 3: Describing Characters
Skill Strand: Creative

____	____	1. Realizing that authors can choose what they describe
____	____	2. Understanding that authors make these choices to tell their readers what they want them to know
____	____	3. Being able to select what to describe and giving the reader the information the reader needs to have

Exercise 4: Conflict
Skill Strand: Creative

Skills   Needs
Mastered   Experience

_____   _____ 1. Understanding that conflicts are important and resolvable
_____   _____ 2. Creating and resolving conflicts in writing

Exercise 5: Point Of View
Skill Strand: Expository

_____   _____ 1. Knowing the choices an author has in his use of point of view
_____   _____ 2. Understanding how these point of view elements work
_____   _____ 3. Understanding the structuring of an explanatory exposition
_____   _____ 4. Writing an explanatory exposition

Exercise 6: What Makes It What It Is
Skill Strand: Creative

_____   _____ 1. Creating, for a reader, the character of a place
_____   _____ 2. Making a reader feel about a place in a desired way

Exercise 7: Survey
Skill Strand: Research

_____   _____ 1. Writing unbiased questions
_____   _____ 2. Selecting a representative sample as respondents to a survey
_____   _____ 3. Taking an oral survey
_____   _____ 4. Reporting on the results of a survey

Exercise 8: Argument
Skill Strand: Expository

_____   _____ 1. Establishing a position on an issue
_____   _____ 2. Interviewing local experts on an issue
_____   _____ 3. Using quotations from experts to support a position
_____   _____ 4. Writing an argumentative exposition

#9 BOOK REPORT

Skill Strand: Research and Report

In this exercise you'll learn that:
1. Many novels are based on the development of characters
2. Characters can be analyzed in the same way they are created
3. Some novels can be understood by an examination of their characters

Most of the books you'll be reading from now on will have characters who change in the ways they think and believe, and the stories will be based on the development of these characters. In this book, report you'll examine and describe the development of the main character or characters.

In the **first section**, you'll introduce to your reader the **book, author, publisher** and publication **date.**

In the **second section** you should let your reader know that the **central idea** in your book is the **development of** the main **character.**

You'll want to describe the character's makeup before the climax and show how the changes are evident because of what happens.

There should be sections taken from the book, in the form of quotations and examples, to support everything you say about the character's development.

Things you should look at for changes are:

1. **Relationships** with other characters
2. **Reactions** to events
3. **Attitudes** toward the things that happen to people and animals
4. **Changes** in the way the character **interacts** with others
5. **Changes in values** or the adoption of **new values**
6. How the character **views himself** or herself

I recommend you take the next week off from writing.

#9 REPORT

Name:_____ Date:_____

Exercise #9: REPORT

Copy your best paragraph for the week on the lines below.

_____

_____

_____

_____

_____

_____

_____

Name one mistake you made this week that you can fix and will avoid next week.

_____

_____

Write the sentence that had this mistake in it.

_____

_____

Write the sentence again showing how you fixed this mistake.

_____

_____

Comments:

#10 BEHAVIOR

Skill Strand: Reporting

It may take you six days to learn to:
1. Observe a situation and take notes so you can write about it
2. Describe what you've seen over a period of days
3. Write a formal scientific report

PREWRITING

Day One:

Sociologists are scientists who study the behavior patterns of groups of people. Sometimes they observe people living on islands or in deserts or jungles, but many times they make their observations in the countryside or in the cities in which they live.

Sociologists, usually working for universities, sometimes make reports on what they observe about the behaviors of people, and they write papers and books about what they've learned. You might be interested in checking the card catalogue in your library under *sociology* for some writings on people's behavior.

You'll be writing a sociological report for this exercise. It will be based on your study of the behaviors of people as they function in groups in your town. One of your parents may ask to be a partner for this work. Often, when sociologists study indigenous groups, they have partners who share the excitement or danger. You'll be going into unknown territories, and you might need some support. You and your partner will have to decide what kinds of group behaviors you'll observe.

Sociologists are not so much interested in individual behaviors. In this exercise you'll be studying the behaviors of groups involved in the rituals of eating. This can be done in any restaurant. You could choose a fast food place and/or a rather expensive lunch room. It might make a nice report for you to observe and report on the differences in the eating habits of the two groups found in these two types of eating places.

In deciding what patterns you and your partner will observe and write about, you might think about this list of possibilities on the next page:

1. Methods of serving and eating the food, which could include:
   A. Selecting from a buffet
   B. Ordering from a waiter, from a menu, a standard lunch or ala carte selections
   C. Ordering at a counter such as is common at fast food places

2. Seating arrangements, which could include:
   A. Stools at a counter
   B. Tables with fixed seats
   C. Individual tables with regular chairs

3. Place service, which could include
   A. Plastic-wrapped plastic utensils
   B. Self serve trays of utensils
   C. Silverware wrapped in paper napkins on a table with paper place mats
   D. Silver service on cloth-covered table with cloth napkins

4. Eating habits, which could include
   A. Talking with full mouths
   B. Sharing food items
   C. Wiping greasy mouths and fingers on shirts and pants
   D. Leaving litter on the tables
   F. Putting refuse in cans
   G. Eating with elbows on the table

There are lots of other things you could observe and write about. You can make your own lists. You parent might want to talk today about some other native customs and primitive practices to be found in restaurants.

Preparation:
You'll prepare for tomorrow:
1. The list of behaviors you'll observe
2. The observation notes you made during your first observation period

WRITING

Day Two:
You should start your paper with a title that tells your reader **who the report is for**, **what group was observed** and **who did the observing**. Your title should look like the one on the next page. Note that the parts of the title are centered, and the small words are not capitalized:

Report to the Sociology Department
of
The University of Non-Such
on the
Differences in Eating Behaviors
of
Patrons of a Fast Food
and a
Medium Priced Restaurant
by
(Phyllis Smith and Mrs. L Smith)

Today you'll write the introduction. This paper will not be like the papers you've written before. You'll write this as if it were a sociological report to a university which has paid for your trip into the Eating Rooms.

The **INTRODUCTION** might include the following information:
1. The **reason** for the study (who wanted to learn what and why)
2. The **importance** of the study (what the scientists hoped would be the value of what was learned—how that information would be used)
3. How the study was **funded** (who paid for it)
4. The **duration** of the study (how long it took)
5. The **general conclusions** of the study (what was learned about the differences in eating behaviors—can be in just one or two sentences and be very general)

There is nothing wrong with telling your reader things like: *This report was commissioned by _____ and your team was ordered to examine the differences in eating habits and behaviors in both a middle class and a fast food restaurant.*

Day Three:

You should have the introduction written and the rough draft of it read by your parent by now. (If not, work harder.)

The **BODY** of your report will consist of the conclusions you've come to and the observations those conclusions were based on. The list of behaviors you made on day one will give you the organization for the body.

Your introduction presents your reader with a general conclusion you've come to from your examination of the natives. The body will give your reader the supportive conclusions upon which this general conclusion was based. This part of your paper might read like the example on the next page:

66

Major Conclusion (stated in the introduction):

There are (or there are not) differences in the eating habits of the natives observed in two different levels of eating places.

Each section of the body should start with a supportive conclusion and that supportive conclusion should support the major conclusion given in the introduction. The first body part can read like this: (You might read that paragraph again.)

Supportive conclusion:

The natives' eating habits in the two levels of eating places were found to be very different, and it does not appear possible that these two groups of eaters would ever be able to eat in the same eating place. The investigators spent two days observing the eating habits of the natives and found the following conditions in the fast food restaurant:

1. *Natives who chew with their mouths open, 34%.*
2. *Natives who talk with food in their mouths, 56%. Sometimes some of this food is even ejected when they laugh or talk loudly. It is sprayed over the tables and other natives.*
3. *Natives who eat with one hand in the lap, 3%.*
4. *Natives who use a napkin to wipe their mouths , 4%.*
5. *Natives yelling across the tables to other natives, 18%.*
6. *Natives who eat with their elbows on the table, 89%.*

There should be the same type of listing for the medium priced restaurant.

Other supportive conclusions can deal with comparisons in such areas as:

1. Types of food eaten
2. Methods of entry into the room
3. Methods of leaving the room
4. Selected partners for the feeding ritual
5. Control of the room by the resident natives
6. Communication techniques during the feeding period

Preparation:
You should prepare a section each day for your parent to read.

Days Four through Six:
When you've finished the last section of your body, your paper will be finished.

Your final paper could be structured to be like this example:

(Your Name, First and Last)
(The Date)

(Skip two spaces)

(The Title of Your Report)
(Skip one Line)
(The Introduction)
1. The **reason** for the study
2. The **importance** of the study
3. How the study was **funded**
4. The **duration** of the study
5. The **general conclusions** of the study
(The Body)   (Skip no Lines)
(Supportive Conclusions)
1.
2.   (Each Supportive conclusion must support the
3.   General Conclusion as stated in the introduction)
4.
5.

(Equal margins on all sides of each page and page # bottom center except for page #1)

I recommend you take the next week off from writing.

PROGRESS REPORT

Name:_____ Date:_____

Exercise #10: BEHAVIOR

Copy your best paragraph for the week on the lines below.

_____
_____
_____
_____
_____
_____
_____
_____

Name one mistake you made this week that you can fix and will avoid next week.

_____
_____

Write the sentence that had this mistake in it.

_____
_____

Write the sentence again showing how you fixed this mistake.

_____
_____

Comments:

69

#11 INTERVIEW WITH A CHARACTER

Skill Strand: Creative

It may take you six days to learn:
1. Imaginary characters must act because of internal motivation
2. You can create an imaginary character and then give it a will of its own
3. The structuring of an interview

PREWRITING

Day One:

One of the very common but important things that newspaper and magazine reporters do is interview people.

A good interview for any purpose is much more complicated than just asking a series of questions of the interviewee. There is research which the interviewer has to do. A reporter must find out all that can be learned about a person before beginning the interview. You might watch Barbara Walters or David Frost do interviews on TV, or you could read interviews of famous people in *Sociology* or *U.S. News and World Report*, three magazines that often have good interviews.

For this exercise you should work with a parent or some other member of your family. You'll transcribe an interview with a character from a novel, fable, myth or short story. In your research for this interview, you'll have to try and determine why the character you've selected acts as he or she does.

Only when you think you know enough about the character to be able to ask penetrating questions, will you be ready to interview that character. It's at this time that your partner can help you. Of course, you'll both have had to read the piece of fiction.

WRITING

You'll have to decide from what writing you're going to select a character to interview and then borrow it from the library if you don't have a copy. You might have to rummage for a story with a character you like enough to study.

After you've finished reading your story, you'll have to do some research on the character for your interview. This outline may help you.

The name of the piece of fiction: _____

Character's name: _____

What this character does for a living or activities engaged M.C.L. the story:

_____

The "problem" in the story: _____

_____

_____

What part does this character play in the solving of this problem?

_____

_____

What makes this character do the things he/she does?

_____

_____

How does this character feel about the way things work out?

_____

You now have to try to think of the questions which will make an interesting interview. The following list of questions may help you:

1. **Who will be the reader** of your interview?
2. What is the **reader's age** and reading background?
3. Will this reader have **read the piece** of fiction that contains the character?
4. Will this reader be **interested** in this character because of the type of **character** it is, or will this reader be interested in the **problem** in the story?
5. What is there about this character that **you find interesting**?

When you have the answers to these questions, the questions you'll ask your interviewee will be easier to write.

Day Two:
Write the questions you'll ask your interviewee. These should not be questions that can be answered by a *yes* or *no*. If they were, it wouldn't make an interesting interview

71

because the questions would be longer than the answers, and your reader will not be interested in the questions but in the answers. The questions should be what are called open-ended. They should be structured so the interviewee has to explain something in the answer. For example:

Q: Mr. Hare, what happened in your childhood that gives you so much confidence in your ability to run fast?

Q: Mr. Tortoise, where did you learn that if you kept working at something you would finally finish it?

Write the questions for your interview on your own paper and set it up like this:

1._____
_____

2._____
_____

3._____
_____

4._____
_____

5._____
_____

Day Three:

You've written the questions for your interview. Today you'll give your questions to your partner and your partner will ask them of you. You'll play the part of the interviewee. For this work it might be good for you to get a tape recorder and record your interview. You might find that you'll want to erase much of it and do it over. Fine. I have done that lots of times. Each time you record a part of your interview over, you'll learn something new about interviewing.

When you're being interviewed by your partner, you'll have to understand the motivations for your character and will have to explain to the interviewer why you feel as you do.

This is the point where you can have fun with the interview. You can be as creative as you like.

I'll give you a **very short example** of what I mean, but then you shouldn't write an interview with this same character. Your interview should be **much more extensive**. Your interview should have a short introduction like the example below.

An Interview
With the Ground Hog
Who
Looked For His Shadow

This interview was conducted in the ravine behind my house on Wright Road, in Niles, Michigan. As February 15th came close, I felt that I had as much of winter as I could stand. I began to wonder how much more of it there would be.

I knew that if a ground hog sees his shadow on the 15th of February, there will be six more weeks of winter. Deep in the ravine, I finally found a ground hog hole beneath a fallen tree. After clearing away some of the snow, I banged on the tree to wake up the ground hog.

A very sleepy animal came slowly out of the hole and looked up at me with one eye still closed.

Q: *Mr. Ground Hog, you may be the one who checks to see if you can see your shadow today. Why are you still asleep?*

G.A.:   *Well, But, a see, there's lots a ground hogs in this woods. I don't hafta do all the work, do I? (The ground hog stretched and yawned here and glanced back down to his hole.) I was the one what looked last year and the year before. That's enough fer any beast. Now, go away and let me get back to sleep, will ya?*

Q: *How do you ground hogs decide which one will be the one to wake up and check for shadows?*

G.H: *We draw lots in the fall.*

Q: *How do you do that?*

G.H: *With chipmunks.*

Q: *You draw chipmunks? How does that work?*

G.H: *Ho boy, you don't know nothin', do ya? No wonder we gotta wake up to tell ya how many more weeks of winter ther'll be. See, we collect a buncha chipmunks and everybody takes one. The one that gets the short chipmunk hasta wake up in February*

73

and check for shadows. How's that? Now, can I get back to sleep?

Q: *Thank you, Mr. Ground Hog.*

The last I saw of that ground hog was when he turned and slid back under the tree and down his hole. We had six more weeks of winter that year, so the sun must have been shining that day.

You can put a short conclusion on your interview, such as I did, if you want to.

Day Four:

You'll ask your partner the questions that you prepared for your interview, and your partner can pretend to be the interviewee and answer. If you don't have a recorder, you can take notes on what your partner says, and you can use what you want of them to write the interview. In this way you'll have practice at both asking and answering interview questions. But, you'll be able to use your partner's imagination along with yours to conduct the interview and to transcribe it from the tape.

Day Five:

Make sure your parent reads your interview today. While you're waiting, you should be writing the introduction. Notice in my example introduction that I indicated when and where the interview takes place, who the interview is with and why I am interested in talking with the interviewee. You should include these four points in your interview:

1. **Who** is the interview with?
2. **When** does it take place?
3. **Where** does it take place?
4. **Why** does it take place?

There is one additional point that could be made in your introduction: you might describe what it was like where the interview took place.

Preparation:

You should rewrite the introduction and the interview using the suggestions your parent gave you today.

Day Six:

Write the conclusion today and ask your parent to read over as much of your work as there is time for. You should start on the final draft of the whole paper. You should prepare the finished copy so that you can give it to your parent on day seven.

I recommend you take the next week off from writing.

PROGRESS REPORT

Name:_____ Date:_____

Exercise #11: INTERVIEW WITH A CHARACTER

Copy your best paragraph for the week on the lines below.

_____
_____
_____
_____
_____
_____
_____
_____

Name one mistake you made this week that you can fix and will avoid next week.

_____
_____

Write the sentence that had this mistake in it.

_____
_____

Write the sentence again showing how you fixed this mistake.

_____
_____

Comments:

#12 PROBLEMS

Skill Strand: Creative

It may take you five days to learn to:
1. Describe a problem a person might have by giving that problem to a character
2. Create character motivation
3. Put a character with a problem in a situation where the reader can see the character working with the problem

PREWRITING

Day One:

Some kids are lucky and they're taught, when they're still very young, how to handle frustration and disappointment. Kids who don't have this skill sometimes do have problems handling their frustrations. Some of their behaviors can make their problems worse. This means that the real loser in the end is the kid who does the acting out.

Many of the situation comedies on television use the trouble characters have solving their problems as a basis for comedic bits. The actors do things when they're frustrated or unhappy that don't solve their problems, but make them worse. Your parent may want to discuss with you some of the popular TV situation comedies and point out some actions that are designed for the TV audience to enjoy by laughter.

Think of all the things that people do to lessen their frustrations that can hurt them: take illegal drugs, drink alcohol, drive fast, get into fights, argue with parents and teachers, cheat on tests, lie to people who trust them and create problems for themselves with their teachers, bosses or the police.

A boy or girl who creates disturbances because of frustration at not being able to solve problems is compounding the problem. Your parent may want to spend some time on this first day talking with you about the trouble some people have of not being able to handle problems. Your parent may have asked you to take notes last week about the problems characters on TV have and how they solve them. You may be asked to notice how people handle problems in real life. These can be as simple as not being able to find a parking place, or how to manage two sacks of groceries and a two-year old while looking for car keys.

If you did take notes, your parent might want you to tell about what you observed.

WRITING

Day Two:

You're to start writing a descriptive piece about a boy or girl who has a problem and what was done because of it.

You can have this person do any of the things I have listed above as not effective or you can have this character do any other kinds of things to solve the problem.

This piece should have the following narrative voice point of view:
- **Third person**
- **Past tense**
- **Limited omniscient in knowledge**
- **Objective in attitude**

It might help you to have a short review:

- **Third person** means that the author creates a narrative voice which is not a central part of the action and talks to the reader using *he, she,* or *they.*

- **Past tense** means that the author has the narrative voice speak as if the action of the narrative had already taken place: *Bill saw the dog*, instead of in present tense which would read *Bill sees the dog.*

- **Limited omniscient in knowledge** means that the author has created a narrative voice which knows what is being thought by the characters and knows what is going on in more than one place at a time. This voice is not limited to what would be known by a person living at that time and watching the action from a real place.

- **Objective in attitude** means that the narrative voice doesn't let the reader know that it cares about what is happening to the characters in the narrative.

Preparation:
List the kinds of things your character does to solve the problem:
1._____
2._____
3._____

77

Day Three:

Start your narrative. Be sure to check exercise #5 if there are any things you don't understand about the point of view.

Ask your parent to read your paper as soon as you have the first paragraph. This may save you lots of work if you're not using the correct point of view.

You'll have to set the scene. Your readers will have to know where and when this action takes place. They'll have to be introduced to the main characters.

You should have a central action that this narrative revolves around. It can be one of the techniques your character employs to solve a problem, or it can be a problem caused by some act that was committed to solve the problem that didn't work and might even have been destructive to the character.

Preparation:
Using your parent's suggestions, rewrite what you wrote in this session. Continue with your writing so that you'll have something new to show your parent as soon as your writing session starts on day four.

Day Four:

Your parent will read your rewritten beginning and your new material and make suggestions. You should be able to finish the rough draft of the exercise today.

Preparation:
Work on making smooth transitions between ideas in your rough copy.

Day Five:

Work on your final copy. Make sure your parent looks at your efforts, for your finished paper is due tomorrow.

I recommend you take the next week off from writing.

PROGRESS REPORT

Name:_____Date:_____

Exercise #12: PROBLEMS

Copy your best paragraph for the week on the lines below.

_____

_____

_____

_____

_____

_____

_____

_____

Name one mistake you made this week that you can fix and will avoid next week.

_____

_____

Write the sentence that had this mistake in it.

_____

_____

Write the sentence again showing how you fixed this mistake.

_____

_____

Comments:

#13 INTERACTIONS

Skill Strand: Creative

It may take you six days to learn how to:
1. Construct an emotional relationship between two people
2. Punctuate dialogue
3. Describe, in a dialogue, characters' major body movements caused by their emotional reactions

PREWRITING

Day One:

One of the marks of maturity is the ability to control the body. The more people develop emotionally, the more they're able to control what they do. We would be very surprised to see the President of the United States lie on the floor and kick his heels, but it would not be surprising to see a two year old do this.

Mature people do react physically when they're upset, and if you understand why and how they do this, you'll be better able to control what your body does.

You may have seen TV or movie characters who have lost control when under emotional strain. This is similar to the way little kids handle their reactions. When these kids get older, they'll be able to handle their emotions in more mature ways.

When people are upset, it affects their bodies, and we can tell how they feel by the ways they move. When people are relaxed, their bodies don't move much at all. When they're bored, they might move a foot or hand or just a finger in repetitive ways. Your parent might call it "jiggling your foot." When people are worried or anxious, they hold and twist things. If there is nothing else handy, they hold and twist their own hands.

When people are ashamed or are being bawled out by a person in authority, like a boss or a parent, and they know that they're guilty of whatever they're being bawled out for having done, they look down to avoid the authority figure's eyes, and they pick at themselves or at their clothing.

80

When some people are upset at other people, they might really like to strike out and hit at them, but they can't do that, or people would all be hurting each other all the time. In extreme cases, less mature people instead hit a table or desk. They kick the chair or rug or dog instead of the person they're upset with. Instead of striking and breaking the person, they throw objects and break things like plates, tools and toys.

WRITING

You'll write a piece of dialogue in which the people are upset with each other. You'll demonstrate for your reader, by how your characters move their bodies, that they're emotional and excited. Create people of different ages so you can show how some people have learned to handle being upset.

It's good to understand how adults handle their bodies during times of emotion and so learn what you can do to improve how you can handle yours. Your parent may want to spend some of this first day talking with you about how and why people get emotional and what they do when this happens.

Days Two through Six:

You'll write a scene between an adult and a teenager who can be 13 or 14 years old. This conversation can take place in a living room, a locker room or in a kitchen in a home, in the teenager's room, or you can have the characters move throughout their house.

You'll have to decide what kinds of people you'll have in your dialogue. You can make the adult be very mature and able to control emotional reactions and you can make the teenager less able at control if you'd like to show the differences. You could have the teenager display emotional reactions and have the adult remain calm and controlled.

You'll have to be careful to not make the adult seem cold. Adults have emotional reactions just like young people do, but sometimes, if they don't show their emotions, young people think they don't have feelings at all.

The important thing in this exercise is that your reader sees the people use their bodies along with their words to express how they feel. It should help you to get started if you first decide what kinds of people you're going to write about. This outline may help:

Teenager's name:_____ Age:_____

Intelligence: Very smart:_____ Average:_____ Dumb:_____

Self control: Can control self: _____ Cannot control self:_____

81

Adult's name:_____ Age:_____

Size: Fat:_____   Thin:_____   Average:_____

Short:_____   Tall:_____   Average:_____

Where the conversation takes place:_____

Who starts the conversation:_____

Which of the characters is good at controlling emotions so that the emotions don't take over and control the body actions:

_____

Remember that when your characters become emotional and they get upset it will affect their bodies. They'll move, and their actions will tell your readers how they feel about the situation. This part of your narrative might read like this:

> The old Buick station wagon crunched in the gravel of the drive. John's head snapped up and he let out a short whoop of excitement, slammed shut the youth group ledger, threw the pencil into the can on the desk and raced for the front of the house. When he hit the living room he almost ran into his mother. "Mom, did you find my waders? They should be in the back of the hall closet," he yelled as he skipped sideways to miss her.
>
> Mrs. Rodgers held her hands in front of her body to protect her from being run into. She laughed and said, "Slow down, John. You'll get to the river before the fish have all gone to bed. I think I just heard your father drive in." She put her hand on John's shoulder and said, "Did you finish the bookkeeping like you promised?"
>
> "Sure. . . Well. . . almost." John was looking back and forth at the hall closet door and his mother's face.
>
> "What does 'almost' mean?" she said as she put one hand under his chin and turned his face so she could look into his eyes.

One of the easiest ways to learn to punctuate dialogue is to pick up any novel and see how that author does it. The rules for this are very standard.

On the next page, I have written a short piece of dialogue as if I were doing this exercise, and you may copy how I have punctuated it if you want to.

Mr. Rodgers threw his jacket over the hall chair, like he did every day, but this time he headed for the stairs. "Hi, Hon, John," he said as he started to climb. "Did you find John's waders?"

"No."

"You check the hall closet?"

"Not yet."

"John, you better find them and load your stuff in the back. I'll be right down. We gotta hurry. That big bass is waiting for us," he said as he slapped the railing.

Mrs. Rodgers was holding her hands in front of her and wringing them lightly, almost as if she were washing them. "William, I think John's got something to talk to you about."

"What?"

"He better tell you."

Mr. Rodgers looked from his wife's eyes to John's and back again. He could see that there was a problem. He stepped back down the three stairs and looked at his son. "What, John?"

Make sure you ask your parent to read your work every day. This is the only way you'll improve.

I recommend you take the next week off from writing.

PROGRESS REPORT

Name:_____ Date:_____

Exercise #13: INTERACTIONS

Copy your best paragraph for the week on the lines below.

_____
_____
_____
_____
_____
_____
_____
_____

Name one mistake you made this week that you can fix and will avoid next week.

_____
_____

Write the sentence that had this mistake in it.

_____
_____

Write the sentence again showing how you fixed this mistake.

_____
_____

Comments:

#14 HE DID IT FIRST

Skill Strand: Creative

It may take you five days to learn that you can:
1. Create a character to be like someone you know
2. Give a character motivations
3. Learn about how people handle themselves from your writing

PREWRITING

Day One:

One of the hardest things young people have to learn is to be responsible for what they do. What is natural for young people to do when they make mistakes is to try and find some external reason that things didn't go well. Children can get away with this when they're little. But, when they get to be nine or ten years old, they have to take responsibility for their mistakes. It no longer is acceptable for them to say things like:

"That's not fair."
"He did it first."
"Everyone else was doing it."
"Why don't you punish them; they were doing it too."

These are voices of children who have not learned to be responsible for what they do. Your parent may want to talk to you about this idea before you start to write.

WRITING

Day Two:

You're to write a dialogue (conversation) between an adult and a teenager. You can set this scene anywhere you like. It can be in the child's home, at a meeting hall or in some public place. In this situation the child has made a mistake and done something dumb, the adult has seen the child do it, but the child will not accept responsibility for what has been done.

These notes may help you to get started:

Child's name: _____

Adult's name and relationship to the child: _____

_____

Place of conversation: _____

What the young person has done: _____

_____

What excuse does the young person use for doing the dumb thing?

_____

How are you going to show that the adult understands that the young person is having trouble accepting responsibility?

_____

_____

How will your piece end? _____

_____

In this exercise you'll have two problems:

1. You'll have to have the young person deny responsibility for what was done.

2. You'll have to have the adult wise enough to understand the young person's problem. The adult will have to know what to say to a person who is not mature enough to admit blame for what was done.

In your scene you should have the adult know what the young person has done. The adult could have seen the act, or the adult could have been told by someone else that the young person has done it. The adult could even have been there when it was done.

Preparation:
Prepare for day three the first part of your scene in which the young person does something dumb and an adult learns about it.

Day Three:
Your parent may want to talk to you about how a wise mother handles her child who has been caught red-handed and still denies guilt or responsibility.

86

Preparation:
Rewrite the beginning of your scene using your parent's comments, and write a first rough draft of the rest of your scene.

(Finishing your writing quickly isn't all that good. Taking your time and making sure you really learn the skills the exercise is designed to give you is _good_. You have a choice: pick that which is not good or that which is good.)

Day Four:

Your parent will look over your work. You should use the time until then checking your spelling and punctuation. Be sure and look up the punctuation of dialogue. When your parent has checked over your paper, you should start on the final draft.

Preparation:
Write the final draft for day five.

Day Five:

Your parent might make copies of your paper and have other members of your family read your dialogues as if they were in a play.

If this is done, you'll be able to tell if your characters are realistic (If they are, your paper should sound as if real people are talking).

I recommend you take the next week off from writing.

PROGRESS REPORT

Name:_____ Date:_____

Exercise #14: HE DID IT FIRST

Copy your best paragraph for the week on the lines below.

_____
_____
_____
_____
_____
_____
_____
_____

Name one mistake you made this week that you can fix and will avoid next week.

_____
_____

Write the sentence that had this mistake in it.

_____
_____

Write the sentence again showing how you fixed this mistake.

_____
_____

Comments:

SECOND SEMESTER REPORT

WRITING SKILLS MASTERY

SEVENTH LEVEL WRITING EXERCISES

Student:_____ Date:_____

Exercise 9: Book Report
Skill Strand: Research and Report

Skills Mastered	Needs Experience	
_____	_____	1. Recognizing that many novels are based on the development of characters
_____	_____	2. Understanding how characters are created by analyzing them
_____	_____	3. Writing a book report based on the development of characters

Exercise 10: Behavior
Skill Strand: Report

_____	_____	1. Observing a situation and taking notes so as to be able to write about it
_____	_____	2. Describing what is seen over a period of days
_____	_____	3. Writing a formal scientific report

Exercise 11: Interview With A Character
Skill Strand: Creative

_____	_____	1. Understanding that imaginary characters sometimes do what they want to do because of their internal motivation
_____	_____	2. Writing an interview

Exercise 12: Problems
Skill Strand: Creative

Skills   Needs
Mastered   Experience

_____   _____ 1. Describing a problem a person might have by giving that problem to a
                     character
_____   _____ 2. Creating character motivation
_____   _____ 3. Putting a character in a situation where the reader can see the character
                     working with the problem

Exercise 13: Interactions
Skill Strand: Creative

_____   _____ 1. Constructing an emotional relationship between two people
_____   _____ 2. Punctuating dialogue
_____   _____ 3. Describing, in a dialogue, characters' major body movements caused by
                     their emotional reactions

Exercise 14: He Did It First
Skill Strand: Creative

_____   _____ 1. Creating a character to be like someone known
_____   _____ 2. Giving a character motivations
_____   _____ 3. Learning about self from writing

COMMON PROBLEMS
with
DEFINITIONS * RULES * EXAMPLES

AMBIGUITY

A statement may be taken in two ways.

1. *She saw the man walking down the street.*

   This can mean either:
   A. *She saw the man when she was walking down the street;* or,
   B. *She saw the man when he was walking down the street.*

2. The use of pronouns *it, she, they, them* that do not have clear antecedents (what they refer to) can create ambiguous sentences:

   Bill looked at the coach when <u>he</u> got the money.

   This can mean either:
   A. *When Bill got the money he looked at the coach;* or,
   B. *Bill looked at him when the coach got the money.*

APOSTROPHE

An apostrophe (') is a mark used to indicate possession or contraction.

Rules:
1. To form the possessive case (who owns it) of a singular noun (one person or thing), add an apostrophe and an *s*.

   Example:

   the girl's coat   Bill's ball   the car's tire

2. To form the possessive case of a plural noun (two or more people or things) ending in *s*, add only the apostrophe.

   Example:

   the boys' car   the cars' headlights

91

3. Do not use an apostrophe for: *his, hers, its, ours, yours, theirs, whose.*

    Example:

    > *The car was theirs.*   *The school must teach its students.*

4. Indefinite pronouns: (could be anyone) *one, everyone, everybody,* require an apostrophe and an *s* to show possession.

    Example:

    > *One's* car is important.   That must be *somebody's* bat.

5. An apostrophe shows where letters have been omitted in a contraction (making one word out of two).

    Example:

    > *can't* for cannot   *don't* for do not   *it's* for it is
    > *we've* for we have   *doesn't* for does not

    Note that the apostrophe goes in the word where the letter or letters have been left out.

6. Use an apostrophe and an *s* to make the plural of letters, numbers and of words referred to as words.

    Example:

    > There are three *b's* and two *m's* in that sentence.
    > It was good back in the *1970's*.
    > Do not say so many "*and so's*" when you explain things.

AWKWARD WRITING

Awkward writing is rough and clumsy. It can be confusing to the reader and make the meaning unclear. Many times just the changing of the placement of a word or the changing of a word will clear up the awkwardness.

If you read your work out loud or have someone else read to it to you and then to listen to what you're saying, you can catch the awkwardness. Remember that you have to read loud enough to hear your own voice.

1. *Each of you kids will have to bring each day each of the following things: pen, pencil and paper.*

This should be rewritten to read:

Each day bring pens, pencils and paper.

2. *The bird flew down near the ground, and having done this, began looking for bugs or worms because it was easier to see them down low than it had been when it was flying high in the sky.*

There are many problems with that sentence. To get rid of its awkwardness, it could be rewritten to read:

The bird, looking for food, swooped low.

Keep in mind that the point of your writing is for you to give your readers information. The simplest way to do this may be the best way.

CLICHÉ

All of us like to use expressions we have heard or read. Many times you'll use expressions in your writing that you won't realize have been used so many times before that they no longer are fresh and exciting for your readers. The best way to avoid this is to read your work aloud and listen for familiar phrases. Omit them.

round as a dollar	*pretty as a picture*	*tall as a tree*
stopped in his tracks	*stone cold dead*	*fell flat on his face*
snapped back to reality	*graceful as a swan*	*stiff as a board*
limber as a willow	*roared like a lion*	*white as a sheet*

Usually the first expressions young writers think of when they write will be clichés. If you think you've heard of an expression before, don't use it.

COMMAS

You can solve most of your comma problems if you read your work out loud and listen to where your voice drops in each sentence. There is where a comma goes. This will work for about 95% of comma placement. This works because commas are needed and used to make clear the meaning in writing. They indicate a pause or a separation of ideas.

Rules:
1. To separate place names—as in an address, dates, or items in a series

2. To set off introductory or concluding expressions
3. To make clear the parts of a compound sentence
4. To set off transitional or non-restrictive words or expressions in a sentence

Examples:

1. *During the day on May 3, 1989, I began to study.*

I had courses in English, math and geography at a little school in Ann Arbor, Michigan.

The parts of the date should be separated by commas, and the courses in this sentence which come in a list should be separated by commas. You have a choice of whether to put a comma before the *and* just prior to the last item on a list.

2. *After the bad showing on the test, Bill felt he had to study more than he had.*

The introduction—*After the bad showing on the test*—to the central idea of this sentence—*Bill felt he had to study more*—is set off from this central idea by a comma.

3. *Bill went to class to study for the test, and I went to the snack bar to feed the inner beast.*

There are two complete ideas here: 1) *Bill went to study*; and, 2) *I went to eat.* These two ideas can be joined in a compound (two or more things put together) sentence if there's a conjunction (*and*, *but*, *though*) between them and they're separated by a comma.

Notice where the comma is placed in the example below.

4. *Bob, who didn't really care, made only five points on the test.*

The central idea of this fourth sentence is that Bob made only five points on the test. The information given that he didn't care is interesting but not essential to the understanding of the main idea of the sentence. The commas indicate that the words between them are not essential to the meaning of the sentence.

COMMA SPLICE

A comma splice is when the two halves of a compound sentence are joined/separated by a comma.

Example:
Bill had to take the test over again, he felt sorry he would miss the party.

A comma splice can be avoided by writing this sentence in one of the five following ways:

1. *Bill had to take the test over again and felt sorry he would miss the party.*

2. *Bill had to take the test over again; he felt sorry he would miss the party.*

3. *Bill had to take the test over again, and he felt sorry he would miss the party.*

4. *Bill had to take the test over again: he felt sorry he would miss the party.*

5. *Bill had to take the test over again. He felt sorry he would miss the party.*

Notice that the punctuation of each of the above examples gives the reader a different idea about Bill and how he felt.

DIALOGUE STRUCTURE and PUNCTUATION

Dialogue is conversation between two or more people. When shown in writing, it refers to the speech or thoughts of characters.

Rules:
Dialogue can occur either in the body of the writing or on a separate line for each new speaker.

Examples:

1. *John took his test paper from the teacher and said to him, "This looks like we'll get to know each other well." The teacher looked surprised and said with a smile, "I hope so."*

2. *John took his test paper from the teacher and said to him, "This looks like you and I'll get to know each other well."*
   The teacher looked surprised and said with a smile, "I hope so."

3. *John took his test paper from the teacher and thought, "This looks like I'll get to know this old man well this year." The teacher looked surprised—almost as if he had read John's mind—and thought, "I hope so."*

FLOWERY WRITING

Some young writers use flowery writing when they want to impress their readers with how many good words they can use to express ideas. This results in the words used becoming more important than the ideas presented.

Rule:
A general rule that should apply is: What you say should be put as simply as possible.

Example:

The red and fiery sun slowly settled into the distant hills like some great, billowing sailing ship sinking beyond the horizon. It cast its pink and violet flags along the tops of the white canvas-clouds where they waved briefly before this ship of light slid beneath the waves of darkness and cast us all, there on the beach, into night.

This is so flowery that it is hard to read without laughing.

It should be rewritten to read:

As the sun set, we remained on the beach, watching the sky darken.

MODIFIER (dangling)
This means that there's nothing for the modifier to modify in the sentence.

Examples:
Getting up, my arms felt tired. (How did the arms get up all by themselves?)

This should read: *When I got up my arms felt tired.*

Coming down the street, my feet wanted to turn into the park. (Again, how did the feet do this?)

This should read: *Coming down the street, I felt as if my feet wanted to turn toward the park.*

Being almost asleep, the accident made me jump. (It's clear the accident could not have been asleep.)

This should read: *I was almost asleep and the accident made me jump.*

OMITTED WORDS

Most of us leave words out of sentences, or leave the endings off of words. You can solve this problem if you read your work out loud and slowly. You must do this slowly enough that you can catch every syllable.

I've had adult students get angry after I have asked them to read what they've written for the fifth or sixth time before they recognized what they had left out.

PARAGRAPH

A paragraph is a sentence or a group of sentences developing one idea or topic.

Rules:
In nonfiction writing, a paragraph consists of a topic sentence which is supported by other sentences giving additional details. A good rule is: A paragraph in this kind of writing should have at least four supportive sentences, making at least five sentences for every paragraph.

> Example:
> **TOPIC SENTENCE**: One sentence that introduces the reader to the main idea of the paragraph.
>
> **PARAGRAPH DEVELOPMENT**: May be made by facts, examples, incidents, comparison, contrast, definition, reasons (in the form of arguments) or by a combination of methods.

PARALLELISM

Parallelism is two or more parts of a single sentence, having equal importance—being structured the same way.

> Examples:
> 1. *We went home to eat and reading*. This should read: *We went home to eat and to read*. This is obvious in such a short sentence, but this is an easy mistake to make when the sentences get complicated.
>
> 2. *There are a number of things that a boy must think about when he is planning to take a bike trip. He must think about checking the air pressure in his tires, putting oil on the chain, making sure the batteries in his light are fresh and to make sure his brakes work properly.*

Notice in this list there's a combination of four parallel participles and one infinitive which cannot be parallel in structure. (This sounds like English-teacher talk.)

What it means is the first three items on the list: (1) *checking,* (2) *putting* (3) *making* are parallel, but the fifth item on the list, (5) *to make,* is not structured the same way, and so this last item is not parallel in structure with the first four items.

This sentence should be rewritten to read: *He must think about **checking** the air pressure in his tires, **putting** oil on the chain, **making** sure the batteries in his light are fresh and **making** sure the brakes work properly.*

PRONOUN REFERENCE and AGREEMENT

To keep writing from being boring, pronouns are often used instead of nouns.

Rules:

It must be clear to the reader which noun the pronoun is replacing. The pronoun must agree in case, gender and number with that noun. The most common error young writers make is with number agreement.

Examples:

Betty and Janet went to the show, but she didn't think it was so good. (It is not clear which girl didn't like the show.)

If a child comes to dinner without clean hands, they must go back to the sink and wash over. (The word *they* refers to "a child" and the number is mixed.)

This should read: *If children come to dinner without clean hands they should go back and re-wash them.*

Both boys took exams but Bob got a higher score on it. (The pronoun *it* refers to the noun *exams* and the number is mixed here.)

Everybody should go to the show, and they should have their tickets handy. (The problem here is that the word *everybody* is singular and the pronouns *they* and there are plural.) The following words are singular and they need singular verbs: *everybody, anybody, each, someone.*

QUOTATION MARKS

Quotation marks are used to indicate exact words or thoughts and to indicate short works and chapters of long works.

Rule: 1. You should put in quotation marks the direct quotation of a person's words. When you use other marks of punctuation with quotation marks: 1) you should put commas and periods inside the quotation marks; and, 2) put other punctuation marks inside the quotation marks if they're part of the quotation; if they're not part of the quotation, you should put them outside of the quotation marks.

Example: *The salesman said, "This is the gum all the kids are chewing."*

Rule: 2. Put in quotation marks the titles of chapters, articles, other parts of books or magazines, short poems, short stories and songs.

Example: *In this magazine there were two things I really liked: "The Wind Blows Free" and "Flowers," the poems by the young girl.*

REDUNDANCY

Redundancy means using different words to say the same thing. The writer does not gain by this, only confuses and bores the reader.

Examples:
I, myself, feel it is true.
It is plain and clear to see.
Today, in the world, there is not room for lack of care for the ecology.

This is an easy mistake to make, and it'll take conscious thought for you to avoid this problem. There are no exercises that you can do which will help: just use care when you're proofreading your work.

SENTENCE

RUN-ON: This is the combining of two or more sentences as if they were one.

Example:
Bill saw that the fish was too small he put it back in the lake and then put a fresh worm on his hook. (This sentence needs to be broken into two sentences by putting a period between *small* and *he*. It could also be correct with a semicolon between *small* and *he*.)

FRAGMENT: This is part of a sentence which lacks a subject or a verb or both.

Check your sentences to make sure they have both subjects and verbs.

Some writers use fragments effectively. You may do this in your creative writing. Avoid using fragments in your expository papers.

Examples:
Fragments can be powerful if used correctly:

When Janet reached her door, she found it was partly open. A burglar! Someone had been in her house and had left the door open.

SENTENCE VARIETY

Young writers have a tendency to structure all or most of their sentences in the same way. You need to give variety to the structuring of your sentences. A common problem for young writers is that of beginning most sentences with a subject-verb pattern.

Examples:
Janet bought a car. The car was blue. It had a good radio. She liked her car and spent a lot of time in it.

These sentences could be re-written and combined so they all do not start with a subject and verb.

The car Janet bought was blue. Because she liked it so much, she spent a lot of time in it.

SUBJECT-VERB AGREEMENT (number)

Closely related words have matching forms, and, when the forms match, they agree. Subjects and their verbs agree if they both are singular or both are plural.

Rules: Singular subjects require singular verbs, and plural subjects require plural verbs.

Singular: *car, man, that, she, he, it*
Plural: *cars, men, those, women, they*
Singular: *The heater was good. The heater works well.*
Plural: *The heaters were good. The heaters work well.*

Most nouns form plurals by adding the letter *s*, as in *bats* and *cats*. The clue is the final *s*.

It is just the opposite with most verbs. A verb ending in *s* is usually singular, as in *puts, yells, is* and *was*.

Most verbs not ending in *s* are plural, as in *they put, they yell*. The exceptions are verbs used with *I* and singular *you: I put, you put*.

Most problems come when there's a phrase or clause between the subject and the verb.

Example:
This red car, which is just one of a lot full of cars, is owned by John and Bob. It is easy for some young writers to think that cars is the plural subject and write the sentence this way: *This red car, which is just one of a whole lot of cars, are owned by John and Bob.*

The subject of this sentence *This red car* is singular; there are just a lot of words between the subject and the verb, and it confuses the number.

TENSE ERROR

Tense errors occur when writers mix past and present tenses and do not have justification for changing from one to the other.

Rules.
1. Present tense is used to describe actions that are taking place at the time of the telling of the event.

    Example: *John is in the house. Mr. Jones lives there.*

2. Past tense is used to describe actions that have already happened.

    Example: *John was in the house. Mr. Jones lived there.*

3. Future tense is used to describe actions that will happen.

    Example: *John will be in the house. Mr. Jones will live there.*

Order Form

To place your *Writing Strands* order, simply fill out this form and send it to us by mail or by fax. If you would like to get your order started even faster, go to the *Writing Strands* website and place your order online at: www.writingstrands.com

		QTY	Total
Writing Strands 1 Oral Work for ages 3-8	$15 ea.	____	_____
Writing Strands 2 About 7 years old	$20 ea.	____	_____
Writing Strands 3 Starting program ages 8-12	$20 ea.	____	_____
Writing Strands 4 Any age after Level 3 or starting program at age 13 or 14	$20 ea.	____	_____
Writing Strands 5 Any age after Level 4 or starting program at age 15 or 16	$20 ea.	____	_____
Writing Strands 6 17 or any age after Level 5	$20 ea.	____	_____
Writing Strands 7 18 or any age after Level 6	$20 ea.	____	_____
Writing Exposition Senior high school and after Level 7	$20 ea.	____	_____
Creating Fiction Senior high school and after Level 7	$20 ea.	____	_____
Evaluating Writing Parents' manual for all levels of *Writing Strands*	$20 ea.	____	_____
Reading Strands Parents' manual for story and book interpretation, all grades	$20 ea.	____	_____
Communication and Interpersonal Relationships Communication Manners (teens)	$20 ea.	____	_____
Basic Starter Set (SAVE $5.00) *Writing Strands 2, Writing Strands 3, Reading Strands* and *Evaluating Writing*	$75 per set	____	_____
Intermediate Starter Set (SAVE $10.00) *Writing Strands 3, Writing Strands 4, Evaluating Writing, Communication and Interpersonal Relationships* and *Reading Strands*	$90 per set	____	_____
Advanced Starter Set (SAVE $30.00) *Writing Strands 5, Writing Strands 6, Writing Strands 7, Writing Exposition, Creating Fiction, Evaluating Writing, Communication and Interpersonal Relationships* and *Reading Strands*	$130 per set	____	_____
Dragonslaying Is for Dreamers – Package 1st novel in *Dragonslaying* trilogy (Early teens) and parents' manual for analyzing the novel.	$18.95 ea.	____	_____
Dragonslaying Is for Dreamers Novel only	$9.95 ea.	____	_____
Axel Meets the Blue Men 2nd novel in *Dragonslaying* trilogy (Teens)	$9.95 ea.	____	_____
Axel's Challenge Final novel in *Dragonslaying* trilogy (Teens)	$9.95 ea.	____	_____
Dragonslaying Trilogy All three novels in series	$25 set	____	_____
Dragonslaying Trilogy and Parents' Manual Three novels plus parents' manual for first novel	$32.99 set	____	_____

SUBTOTAL (use this total to calculate shipping) _____

Texas residents:	Add 8.25% sales tax	_____
All Orders Shipping:	Add $6 for orders $75 and under	_____
	Add $8 for orders over $75	_____
Canada Shipping:	Add $6	
Outside US/Canada Shipping:	Add $14	_____

TOTAL U.S. FUNDS _____

Mail your check or money order or fill in your credit card information below:

☐ VISA   ☐ Discover   ☐ Master Card

Account Number _____

Expiration date: Month _____ Year _____

Signature **X** _____

We ship UPS to the 48 states, so please no P.O. Box addresses.
PLEASE PRINT

Name _____

Street _____

City _____ State ____ Zip _____

Phone (_____) _____

Email _____

SHIPPING INFORMATION
CONTINENTAL U.S.: We ship via UPS ground service. Most customers will receive their orders within 10 business days.

ALASKA, HAWAII, U.S. MILITARY ADDRESSES AND US TERRITORIES: We ship via U.S. Priority Mail. Orders generally arrive within 2 weeks.

OUTSIDE U.S.: We generally ship via Air Mail. Delivery times vary.

RETURNS
Our books are guaranteed to please you. If they do not, return them within 30 days and we'll refund the full purchase price.

PRIVACY
We respect your privacy. We will not sell, rent or trade your personal information.

INQUIRIES AND ORDERS
Phone:	(800) 688-5375
Fax:	(888) 663-7855 TOLL FREE
Write:	*Writing Strands* 624 W. University, Suite 248T Denton, TX 76201-1889
E-mail:	info@writingstrands.com
Website:	www.writingstrands.com

TO ORDER EVEN FASTER, GO ONLINE AT:
www.writingstrands.com

Prices valid through 3/31/08